BECOMING JEFFERSON

MY LIFE AS A FOUNDING FATHER

Bill Barker

THE COLONIAL WILLIAMSBURG FOUNDATION
WILLIAMSBURG, VIRGINIA

The publication of this book was made possible by
a generous gift from Scott and Debra Duncan.

© 2019 by The Colonial Williamsburg Foundation
All rights reserved. Published 2019

Designed by Katherine Jordan and Ben Cochran

Library of Congress Cataloging-in-Publication Data

Names: Barker, Bill, 1953– author.
Title: Becoming Jefferson : my life as a Founding Father /
    by Bill Barker.
Description: Williamsburg, Virginia : The Colonial
    Williamsburg Foundation, 2019.
Identifiers: LCCN 2018036865 | ISBN 9780879352967
    (hardcover : alk. paper)
Subjects: LCSH: Jefferson, Thomas, 1743-1826. | Historical
    reenactments. | Barker, Bill, 1953– | Actors—United States—
    Biography. | Colonial Williamsburg (Williamsburg, Va.)
Classification: LCC E332.2 .B25 2019 | DDC 973.4/6092—dc23
    LC record available at https://lccn.loc.gov/2018036865

Colonial Williamsburg is a registered trade name of
The Colonial Williamsburg Foundation, a not-for-profit
educational institution.

The Colonial Williamsburg Foundation
PO Box 1776
Williamsburg, VA 23187-1776
colonialwilliamsburg.org

Printed in China

30 29 28 27 26 25 24 23 22 21 20 19   2 3 4 5 6

"Meeting Bill is as close to meeting Thomas Jefferson as you can get."

~ Early American Life

Bill Barker first portrayed Thomas Jefferson in 1981 at Independence Hall in Philadelphia, and he has been a historical interpreter with Colonial Williamsburg since 1993. He has appeared as Jefferson in many other venues as well, including at the White House and the Palace of Versailles, and on ABC, NBC, CBS, PBS, CNN, and the History Channel.

*To the past, present, and future
historical actor–interpreters.*

CONTENTS

PREFACE   8

PART I: JEFFERSON AND ME

Families   14
From Philadelphia to Williamsburg   22
Reading about Jefferson   29
Jefferson in Williamsburg   35

PART II: INTERPRETING

Rehearsing and Improvising	50
Sources	57
Interpretation and Diplomacy	63
Connecting with the Audience	68
Making History Relevant	76
Talking to Kids	82
Teaching Teachers	88
Mr. President	90
Interpreters of the Future	96
Becoming Jefferson, Being Myself	102

PART III: LEGACIES

Gardens	108
Wine	113
Militia	119
The White House	127
Traveling	135
Education	139
Slavery	146
The Bible	156

SOME FINAL THOUGHTS   162

PREFACE

"A morsel of genuine history, a thing so rare as to be always valuable."

~ Thomas Jefferson to John Adams,
8 September 1817

The art of explaining history through the medium of theater has been practiced from the time of the ancients. Yet the art of historical interpretation through interactive first-person portrayals is still very much in its pioneering stage. There is not yet an academic discipline incorporating it.

There is no doubt that elements of theater can transport an audience back in time, enticing them to realize that the characters themselves have no idea what will occur next and perhaps to realize that the same is true today. Historical interpretation at its best creates an intimate and personal touch, an empathy for our past, a direct connection to our history, a recognition that the people of the past were no less intelligent than we are today though they were bound by habits, customs, burdens, and investments of their time.

The first living history museums to engage historical interpreters were Colonial Williamsburg, Plimoth Plantation and Old Sturbridge Village in Massachusetts, and Old Salem in North Carolina, in the mid to late 1980s. Others followed in America and abroad. There are now living history museums in Canada, Ireland, Scotland, England, France, Denmark, Norway, and the Czech Republic among others. Colonial Williamsburg has remained at the forefront of the field.

As for Jefferson, during the last thirty years, several persons have appeared on our national stage in the guise of our third president. The market is hardly crowded, certainly not compared to the Association of Lincoln Presenters, which numbers several hundred. Most of the current Jeffersons know one another and are familiar with each other's work. We also recognize, to our great relief, that we are entirely different in our approaches and methods.

I first appeared as Thomas Jefferson for Colonial Williamsburg in the spring of 1993. I was brought in from Philadelphia to propose a toast to legendary newsman David Brinkley upon his retirement as president of the Colonial Williamsburg Raleigh Tavern Society. During that April weekend, I also portrayed Jefferson in scenes filmed at the Governor's Palace for a testimonial to honor former American ambassador to Great Britain Walter H. Annenberg. One month later, I was invited to be part of special summer programming honoring the 250th anniversary of Jefferson's birth. At the end of August, I was asked if I would be interested to continue in persona as Jefferson and become part of the interpretive programming at Colonial Williamsburg. I did not hesitate. I was already hooked.

What does it mean to interpret Thomas Jefferson? How has that interpretation evolved over three decades?

Thomas Jefferson was Colonial Williamsburg's first consistent "brand-name" historical character, the first to walk the streets of the restored colonial capital of Virginia, the first to become involved in outreach to teachers and students and with donors on cultural expeditions. Since that first summer, Jefferson has participated in, and continues to participate in, archaeological and garden programs and visits to sites throughout the Historic Area, throughout the nation, and in England, Italy, and France.

The eighteenth-century city of Williamsburg provided the young Thomas Jefferson with the opportunity to expand his horizons when he first came to town as a student at the College of William and Mary. Though I arrived in Williamsburg much older, it has provided for me the same setting in history, scholarship, and public service. For more than twenty-five years, I've worked to expand the art of historical interpretation and specifically my interpretation of Mr. Jefferson.

Throughout these years, certain questions have remained in the forefront: What is the art of historical interpretation? How do you blend the elements of theater with real historical accounts to create historical interpretation that is accurate and engaging? How did Jefferson's experiences in Williamsburg influence him throughout his life? And how has our understanding of Jefferson evolved over the years?

I trust what follows may suggest some answers.

———

PREFACE

PART I

JEFFERSON AND ME

FAMILIES

My first trip to Williamsburg was in the womb. My parents visited in the late fall of 1952, when my mother was pregnant with me. Though I was born and grew up in Philadelphia, I am of southern heritage. My father started out as a tenth-generation tobacco farmer, born on a family farm in North Carolina. That farm had been settled by his direct male ancestor in the mid-eighteenth century. My mother's family is from Philadelphia. As my brothers and I were growing up, we visited family in North Carolina every year—and stopping in Williamsburg was always a given.

Mr. Jefferson probably also accompanied family to Williamsburg as a boy. Jefferson's father, Peter Jefferson, was a colonel of Virginia militia, a vestryman of the Church of England, a surveyor often commissioned by the royal governors of Virginia, and a member of the Virginia House of Burgesses. He frequently traveled to Williamsburg for meetings of the House of Burgesses and for submitting survey patents. Most likely young Tom went along on some of these trips.

Though Thomas Jefferson's childhood seems to have been a happy one for him, there were also times of great sadness. He was only fourteen when his father, who was but forty-nine, died suddenly in August 1757. I can relate to that. I lost my father when I was a young boy, and I still feel the pangs of loss and recall the vivid uncertainty and the unanswered questions that followed. Imagine how the young Thomas Jefferson must have felt as the eldest son now responsible for his mother and nine siblings. Jefferson was born into a family of considerable means, and no doubt he had a great deal of help from his capable mother, Jane Jefferson, and servants and slaves, but his father's death would remain a great loss.

He also suffered the loss of two of his siblings when he was a young man. At twenty-two, he lost Jane, his eldest sister, when she was just twenty-five years old. And at the age of thirty, he lost his sister Elizabeth when she was but twenty-nine.

At twenty-eight, he married Martha Wayles Skelton, a widow, and we know he remained deeply devoted to her. She passed away at thirty-three, in September 1782, only ten years into the marriage. They lost three of their six children in infancy, and it was the birth of their sixth child that led to Martha's death. The more one learns of Jefferson's youth, the more you sense his continual experience with personal loss. Inconsolable upon the occasion of his wife's passing, for two weeks he was known to have trod the floorboards of his bedroom with hardly any sleep.

Nearly two years after his wife's death, Jefferson was appointed U.S. minister plenipotentiary to France. His five years in France—from 1785 to 1789—revitalized him. And yet, while he was abroad, his youngest daughter, Lucy Elizabeth, whom he had left under the care of his wife's sister in Virginia, passed away at the age of two.

As fate would have it, his eldest child, Martha, had twelve children, eleven of whom survived to adulthood. His other surviving child, Polly, had three, though only one survived infancy. But, in 1804, when Polly was twenty-five and while Jefferson was president, she died suddenly. The acute sense of loss continued to follow him into adulthood.

Advancing in years and surrounded by grandchildren, Jefferson commented on his remaining child, Martha: "My evening prospects now hang on the slender thread of a single life. Perhaps I may be destined to see even this last cord of parental affection broken!"

In the autumn of 1825, his son-in-law, Martha's husband, Thomas Mann Randolph, who was the manager of Monticello plantation, called Jefferson into the farm office and informed him that there was no way out of his increasing debt. They must consider selling Monticello. Jefferson's eyes welled up. He did not say a word. He raised himself from the chair, feebly, and walked out of the room. From that moment on, it is said, his health began to deteriorate at a steady pace until he passed away on the fourth of July 1826. Randolph's report must have struck a heavy chord of woe, adding to that sense of loss he had experienced so profoundly throughout his life.

My own family history, on the Barker side, goes back to the first families of Virginia, though we rarely spoke of it.

My father, for whom I am named, did not have an extensive formal education. But he nonetheless provided me with a strong connection to our family history. Our family was part of the great southside migration of Virginia families that occurred before the American Revolution. Virginians moved into northern North Carolina seeking virgin soil to cultivate tobacco and seeking to acquire larger tracts of land than they would inherit as younger sons because of the British custom of primogeniture and entail.

▸ FAMILIES

The circa 1764 Barker family homestead in North Carolina.

My father was born in 1894. His paternal line first settled on Jamestown Island and later Surry County, Virginia. His upbringing was a way of life that had not changed much for centuries. He grew up without plumbing or electricity. When, as children, my brothers and I visited our Carolina relations, the roads were still mainly dirt and gravel, the same as when my father's grandfather was born, well before the Civil War.

During these wonderful family visits in a country vastly different from the suburbs of Philadelphia in which I was growing up,

PART I: JEFFERSON AND ME

I loved to roam through the old graveyards and walk about old family homesteads. My father and his brothers and sisters would often point out, "This is where so and so was buried," since many graves were devoid of markers. My mother would then pull out a pencil and paper and tell me to jot down that oral history. Because of those occasions and the remarks of those who are now long gone, I am still able to remember who was buried in those graves.

We are prone to forget, and family history, passed along for several generations, may cease to be valid or readily recalled if one generation forgets or becomes disinterested. The same holds true for history in general: if we forget the past, we will repeat the same mistakes as were made in the past.

Growing up, I loved hearing family stories. It was only natural that I too took an interest in telling stories about history. I loved going to historically based movies, like *Spartacus* and *Mutiny on the Bounty*, reveling in the fascinating storylines and identifying the real history.

Clearly, from my parents I inherited not only a love of history but also a love of storytelling. My father, a farm boy, had a wonderfully relaxed and rambling method of telling a story. My mother, a city girl from Philadelphia who had been educated at Mount Holyoke College in Massachusetts, took a more direct, urbane approach.

▸ FAMILIES

My parents enjoyed traveling, and we would often stop at historic sites. When I was eight years old, my parents took my brothers and me to Monticello. The house immediately caught my fancy and spurred my interest in Thomas Jefferson. Who was this individual who created this delightfully curious house, which was—and still is—so very interesting from every angle, not only out of doors but with an intriguing and intimate labyrinth of connecting rooms and hallways? Who was this person who lived amongst all these fascinating gadgets?

On this first visit to Monticello, I remember vividly that it began to storm, and my father suggested that we immediately get on the road and proceed on to North Carolina. My mother, however, didn't want to leave before taking my two younger brothers and me down to see the Jefferson family graveyard. My father was able to lasso my brothers into the car, but my mother held onto me. In pouring rain, my mother took me down a dirt path to where Thomas Jefferson is buried, and we stood gazing at the tombstone through the large wrought-iron fence. I asked if that was really where he was buried, and my mother replied, "Yes, this is where he lies." That scene still comes back to me, every once in a great while, in my dreams.

Anabel and William Barker behind the Williamsburg Inn in fall 1952.

▸ FAMILIES

From PHILADELPHIA *to* WILLIAMSBURG

Throughout elementary school, high school, and college, one subject and one extracurricular activity drew my interest and energy—history and theater. In the spring of 1980, a friend of mine who was a teacher of Pennsylvania history in Philadelphia and moonlighted interpreting William Penn asked me, "Barker, did anyone ever tell you that you look like Thomas Jefferson?"

He knew I was an actor and he knew I loved history. He told me they needed someone to portray Jefferson at Independence Hall for photo ops and celebrations.

In 2004, historical interpreters in Williamsburg re-created the committee that met in Philadelphia in 1776 to draft the Declaration of Independence: (left to right) Jefferson, Roger Sherman (portrayed by Ron Carnegie), Benjamin Franklin (Ron Warren), John Adams (Steve Holloway), and Robert Livingston (Alex Morse).

In front of Independence Hall in Philadelphia.

No other subject could have been more interesting to me! My first appearance and interpretation as Thomas Jefferson was at Independence Hall. Hobart Cawood was superintendent then, and Frances Delmar, assistant superintendent, became a warm and influential mentor to me.

I knew the answers to a good many of the more popular questions I was asked about Jefferson. However, the profound setting moved me to research his history more thoroughly. I learned to recite passages from his letters and public papers. Soon, tour groups in Philadelphia began hiring me for special occasions, and I began to perform alongside the well-known William Sommerfield as George Washington and Ralph Archbold as Benjamin Franklin. In 1992, I was chosen by the city of Philadelphia to host its yearlong celebrations commemorating the two hundredth anniversary of the Bill of Rights. For more than a decade, I enjoyed developing a repertoire of Jefferson-related theatrical scenarios in Philadelphia. Coincident with this, I pursued a livelihood in theater and was artistic director of the Savoy Company of Philadelphia, the world's oldest continuously performing Gilbert and Sullivan troupe. Gilbert and Sullivan remains a passion of mine, and I firmly believe Mr. Jefferson would have been a devotee of their art.

When I came to Colonial Williamsburg to perform as Thomas Jefferson in the late spring of 1993, there was no consistently performing Founding Father. At the time, there were two concerns about having one. First, the story of the town and its people might be overshadowed by a renowned historical figure. Second, interpreters portraying Washington, Jefferson, or Patrick Henry might be too constrained by the documentation about what famous founders said or did. Lesser-known townspeople allowed interpreters more freedom to interact with visitors. Bringing in a full-time universally and historically well-documented figure like Thomas Jefferson was a risk. And, I was also an outsider!

But by the end of the summer, I had developed many friendships with coworkers, and attitudes began to change. People came to recognize that interpreting Jefferson as a full-time, historical persona in Williamsburg was not only historically valid, it was also another way to recognize Williamsburg's importance in paving the way towards the American Revolution and much of what took place in the Continental Congress in Philadelphia.

Within the next ten years, this approach was expanded to include other Founding Fathers such as Washington, Henry, Madison, and Monroe. Later still it was expanded to include others who built our nation, such as Gowan Pamphlet, the black Baptist preacher; Edith Cumbo, a free African American; and the marquis de Lafayette, whose support was crucial to the success of the Revolution.

Over the quarter century that I have pursued my vocation in Williamsburg, I have not completely severed my connections to Philadelphia, which, indeed, has plenty of connections to Jefferson. There is Independence Hall, of course, and there is Congress Hall, where he served as secretary of state and as vice president. And there is old Laurel Hill Cemetery on the east bank of the Schuylkill River, where my mother's family have

been buried for several generations. Our family would visit there several times a year while I was growing up.

I didn't realize it at that time, but later, after taking up portraying Thomas Jefferson, I began to recognize that many names amongst the tombstones have connections to Jefferson. Not far from where my family were buried rests Jonathan Williams, whom Jefferson appointed as the first superintendent of West Point. In another section of the cemetery is the John Dunlap family. Dunlap produced the first printed versions of the Declaration of Independence. Then there are Henry Voigt, the horologist who made the great clock in the entrance hall at Monticello at Mr. Jefferson's request, and William Duane, the newspaperman, whose *Aurora* encouraged support for Jefferson. William Short, a graduate of William and Mary and Mr. Jefferson's close friend, protégé, and personal secretary during his five years in France, also spends eternity within the grounds of America's second oldest planned rural cemetery, founded in 1836. Mount Auburn Cemetery near Boston was the first, founded in 1831. In 2010 I created a tour, "The Worlds of Thomas Jefferson in Laurel Hill Cemetery." I continue to lead the tour every September or October.

READING *about* JEFFERSON

Jefferson said, "I cannot live without books."

To confirm that Jefferson said this, or to look up the titles of the books Mr. Jefferson read, we have information immediately at our fingertips. We can visit the world's greatest librarian, Mr. Google. But the physical sensation of holding a book in your hands, the opportunity to turn the pages and read—particularly if you are able to hold a book that was published in the seventeenth or eighteenth century—pulls you closer to Mr. Jefferson's sentiments and his world.

In the study of the George Wythe House.

The first books I had the pleasure to read were, naturally, kids' books. They were books that excited the imagination, and later I progressed easily into books that excited my imagination—King Arthur and the Knights of the Round Table, anything about Pompeii and the ancient Roman world, the story of the Titanic with its many connections to Philadelphia. I also enjoyed reading the pamphlets and guidebooks from the historic places our family visited. I still have many of them. One of my early interests was the Civil War, since my father often spoke about both of his grandfathers, whom he knew well and who were both Civil War army veterans. Daddy would frequently refer to them when we visited Gettysburg and other Civil War sites.

I was about eleven or twelve when I first read about Thomas Jefferson. I remember realizing that Jefferson had lived well before the Civil War and yet his connection to the American Revolution was relevant to what eventually brought on the War between the States. Our early trips to Williamsburg also helped clarify that connection since Williamsburg was the scene of a battle during the Civil War. I became fascinated by the idea of the span of history and the connections between different eras.

In college, I read history as a major and focused mainly on American civilization. Recognizing my particular interest in Jefferson, a college friend gave me a compendium of Jefferson letters and papers, which I still have. Over the years, I continue to refer to this book.

In 1974, Fawn Brodie's book *Thomas Jefferson: An Intimate History* quickly became a best seller. I first read it in 1976 when I was working in the furniture department at the Strawbridge & Clothier department store in Jenkintown, Pennsylvania. During moments of retail inactivity, I would read Brodie's book. On one occasion the store manager caught me and warned me that reading did not constitute selling furniture. I couldn't stop. The third time he caught me, I was fired.

Fawn Brodie's was a beguiling and intense book. It still is, though its psychological approach was very much a product of its time. The furor of national attention that it spurred led to the eventual DNA investigations into Jefferson-Hemings family ties. In 1998, the results of that science proved a distinct blood relation between Thomas Jefferson and Sally Hemings's last child, Eston Hemings, who was born in 1808.

My continuing study of Jefferson remains as fascinating and enjoyable as the theatrical portrayals. I have always been a victim of too much imagination, and I can't get enough of the past: What were people and moments in history really like? I remain intrigued by the idea of going back in time—to the real, living, breathing past. What would be the frame of mind? What would be the day-to-day differences in the way of life, the habits, the customs, the tastes, and the extent of knowledge of the world and the universe?

Stepping into the Historic Area of Colonial Williamsburg provided me the opportunity not only to step back into a semblance of a way of life over two hundred years ago but especially to

view that world more so through Jefferson's eyes. Colonial Williamsburg not only allowed me to perform as Jefferson every day but also to continue to read and read and read. This opportunity helped to substantiate the facts of Mr. Jefferson's life and to reveal new discoveries about him and his eighteenth-century world.

This wonderful oyster continues to be precious to me—as was the setting to Jefferson and Washington and Madison and Henry. They not only performed on the historical stage of Williamsburg,

▸ READING ABOUT JEFFERSON

but they took the time to read the provocative authors of their own time—John Locke, Isaac Newton, Sir Francis Bacon, Rousseau, Voltaire, Montesquieu—to understand how history affected their responsibilities to public service. Their opinions, even when they disagreed, were grounded in historical precedence. They drew on the wisdom of the ages to create a new government and a new system of laws. Their reading was vital to what they were accomplishing.

In 2016, Colonial Williamsburg, aware that the art of historical interpretation has become a valid method of teaching history while breathing life into our eighteenth-century buildings and along Duke of Gloucester Street, began to pursue a method of sustaining living history by auditioning the persona of a young Thomas Jefferson. For several years now, it has been my delightful experience to work with Kurt Smith, mentoring him as he has taken on the Jefferson persona. Kurt has a desk at Colonial Williamsburg's Rockefeller Library that is covered with books. His portrayal continually becomes more substantiated by his study. After twenty-five years of presenting Thomas Jefferson at Colonial Williamsburg, it is immensely rewarding to see Kurt Smith's ever-evolving personal enlightenment as he hones his craft.

JEFFERSON *in* WILLIAMSBURG

The earliest correspondence we have of Jefferson's is a January 1760 letter he wrote to the executors of his father's estate. In it, he argued that he should be allowed to continue his education, which had included in part the reading of books in his father's library. In particular, he wished to go to the College of William and Mary in Williamsburg.

He suggested that this opportunity would allow him to make himself worthy as the inheritor of his father's estate. He was then sixteen years old.

Members of the House of Burgesses met in the Apollo Room at the Raleigh Tavern in 1769 and signed a nonimportation agreement to protect British policies.

Jefferson arrived in Williamsburg in March of that same year and enrolled for the spring semester. He lived on the top floor of the college building with other students, a sort of dormitory, for the first semester or two. Later he rented rooms in town at Thomas Craig's tavern on Market Square. He also stayed with his cousin Peyton Randolph on occasion.

Of his early days in Williamsburg, he wrote:

> When I…recollect the various sorts of bad company with which I associated from time to time, I am astonished I did not turn off with some of them and become as worthless to society as they were. I had the good fortune to become acquainted very early with some characters of very high standing, and to feel the incessant wish that I could ever become what they were. Under temptations and difficulties, I would ask myself what would Dr. Small, Mr. Wythe, Peyton Randolph do in this situation? What course in it will ensure me their approbation? I am certain that this mode of deciding on my conduct tended more to its correctness than any reasoning powers I possessed. Knowing the even and dignified line they pursued, I could never doubt for a moment which of two courses would be in character for them. Whereas seeking the same object through a process of moral reasoning, and with the jaundiced eye of youth, I should often have erred.

These three highly respected men, whom Jefferson knew personally in Williamsburg, remained influential throughout his entire life.

My initial experience portraying Jefferson in Williamsburg was not unlike what I had already experienced in Philadelphia and Washington. There were formal presentations and speeches followed by questions from the audience. However, walking down Duke of Gloucester Street every day and creating chance encounters with guests resulted in a different kind of theatrical experience. This day-to-day interpretation is something I savor and enjoy as an actor and as a historian. There is no script. It is entirely extemporaneous. It is the art of interpretive historical improvisation.

For me, one of the delightful sentiments about interpreting Jefferson in Williamsburg is being in Jefferson's element. There is a modern presence of course—paved roads, electricity, plumbing, air-conditioning being obvious examples—but, as an entire re-created eighteenth-century town, it is vastly different from any other historical venue in the world. It is certainly a privilege to portray Jefferson in Independence Hall. I continue to be mesmerized by all the history that occurred in that building. I remain awed by the realization that the floorboards are the very ones Jefferson walked upon, the windows the very same through which he gazed. I will always be proud to be known as a son of

Philadelphia. But you walk out of Independence Hall to cars and buses driving up and down Chestnut Street. Granted, maybe there will be a horse-drawn carriage or two, but the modern glass and brick pavilion through which the Liberty Bell may be seen reminds us overwhelmingly of a progressing modern world.

Walk out of the George Wythe House, where Jefferson spent much time, onto Palace Green, and you see pretty much what Jefferson saw. The catalpa tree–lined green, the imposing Governor's Palace, and the handsome Robert Carter House and quaint Thomas Everard House on either side of the Palace, all wonderfully maintained in their eighteenth-century setting. Both inside and out, Colonial Williamsburg's Historic Area resembles the town as Jefferson knew it, a place and its people that were incredibly influential during twenty years of his youth, a place he experienced as the capital of the largest colony of the British Empire and then as the capital of the commonwealth of Virginia. The twenty years Jefferson was active on the scene in Williamsburg, 1760–1780, as student, lawyer, burgess, delegate, and governor, would indeed remain his oyster for the rest of his life.

We learn of Jefferson's general impressions of Williamsburg in his *Notes on the State of Virginia*, first published in 1785, as well as in his correspondence. In *Notes*, he is not flattering in his overall appraisal. He called the college and hospital buildings "rude, misshapen piles, which, but that they have roofs, would be taken for brick kilns." Perhaps Jefferson was influenced by the elegant architectural renderings in James Gibbs's *A Book of Architecture, Containing Designs of Buildings and Ornaments* and Robert Morris's *Select Architecture*, which were his first books on the subject and which he acquired in Williamsburg while he was a student there.

I remember learning, around the age of eleven, that Jefferson had lived in the Governor's Palace when he served as the second governor of the Commonwealth of Virginia. How immense the

Governor's Palace appeared in comparison with Monticello. Many think of Monticello as a large house, and in its day it was considered so. However, Jefferson's genius in architectural design resulted in an elegant grand house that is beautifully compact with very intimate sections. His later design for his retreat house at Poplar Forest is even more perfect in its elegant cohesion of intimate rooms. The idea of a retreat is a recurring theme throughout Jefferson's life; he continually sought a place where he could be alone to read, write, and simply think.

Jefferson's early influences in the art of architecture were derived from his acquaintance with several of the magnificent early Virginia plantation houses, such as Westover, Berkeley, Shirley, and Rosewell. However, he never forgot the warmth of the family bond, and he appreciated an intimate space amidst beautifully elegant surroundings, both indoors and out.

Jefferson did not care for the Palace's immense, drafty rooms. The Governor's Palace, which many think elegant, he considered "not handsome without: but it is spacious and commodious within, is prettily situated, and with the grounds annexed to it, is capable of being made an elegant seat." He thought its design would serve better as an elegant country seat; in Williamsburg, it overwhelmed the surrounding buildings. He suggested a redesign of the Palace when he lived there only a short time as governor. To make it more intimate, he suggested removing the

In the Governor's Palace garden.

grand staircase and dividing the ballroom into two separate chambers. Of course, early Virginia officials never intended it to be warm and cozy—it was supposed to be imposing as a symbol of royal authority.

Another structure in town with a Jefferson connection is Market Square Tavern. We know from his memorandum books that he stayed here on occasion while a student at the college and later while reading the law with George Wythe. Close by, on Market Square, is the Magazine, built well before Jefferson's time and still in use to store the colony's weapons and munitions while he was here. And, of course, there is the Capitol at the east end of Duke of Gloucester Street where, as a student in 1765, he overheard Patrick Henry's impassioned words in the House of Burgesses over the Stamp Act and where he himself sat as a burgess and also argued cases before the General Court after receiving his law license.

Jefferson's cousin Peyton Randolph lived in the imposing house that today carries his name. Jefferson felt at home there, enjoying the company of extended family. Peyton was the son of Sir John Randolph, Jefferson's mother's uncle. Jefferson's grandfather, Isham Randolph, was Sir John Randolph's brother. Their father and mother, William and Mary Randolph, had seven sons and three daughters, and have often been referred to as the Adam and Eve of Virginia gentry.

Jefferson frequently visited George Wythe's house on Palace Green as a student. He read law with Mr. Wythe for three years after he left the College of William and Mary in 1762. Jefferson called George Wythe "my faithful and beloved mentor in youth, and my most affectionate friend through life."

Next to the Wythe House is Bruton Parish Church, in which Jefferson worshipped during his twenty years in Williamsburg. Many of the tombstones in the graveyard mark the passing of people who died during Jefferson's time in town. He surely was familiar with many of them, particularly Francis Fauquier, royal lieutenant governor of Virginia, who is buried inside the church, and James Nicholson, steward of the College of William and Mary.

The William Finnie House on the south side of Francis Street has an interesting Jefferson connection. Some regard it as a prototype for the first Monticello, before it was remodeled and enlarged. It certainly is very similar. Monticello as Jefferson originally designed it was very different from how it looks today. To envision the first Monticello mansion, picture the Finnie House's two-story central section, to which Jefferson, in the original Monticello, added a colonnade and balcony to both the front and the back. Then envision the same side appendages as well. Was this a coincidence? Or was it a studied remembrance with improvements?

In the study of the Peyton Randolph House.

The capital was moved to Richmond in 1780. In this scene, Jefferson prepares to leave the Governor's Palace.

Jefferson was known to have referred to Williamsburg as a capital of hospitality, education, and good manners. This contrasts decidedly with earlier references in the correspondence of his youth where he refers to the capital as "Devilsburg." Certainly there were all sorts of devilment going on in the social and political center of the colony. Gossip and intrigue were to be expected. But we should not forget that he was still a teenager and a student at the college when he applied that description to the capital city.

PART I: JEFFERSON AND ME

The Williamsburg Jefferson knew was a grimy city, its streets spotted with horse dung and the air permeated with smells of chimney smoke, cookery, and animals. Its population in 1775 was close to two thousand. Add to that the many who arrived for court days, market days, and sessions of the legislature—along with the increase in number of horses and other livestock. Consider as well that there was no sewage system! Instead, there were outhouses, or *necessaries*, to use the period term, on private properties and public sites throughout the city. Likely human waste from chamber pots was also thrown into the streets.

Nor were buildings as pristine as we see them today. Many were not painted, and there were more outbuildings: necessaries, dairies, smokehouses, and stables. The streets were dirt or, depending on the weather, mud. There were few lawns and fewer trees within the city. And you wouldn't have found lovely landscaped gardens behind every house. More often there were dirt or what were called "swept dooryards" along with vegetable gardens. Also abundant were chickens, dogs, cats, and cows. And there was a tannery on the outskirts of town. When the wind shifted, its scent spiked the air.

This was the Williamsburg with which Jefferson was well-acquainted. It was the city to which he traveled repeatedly in his youth in pursuit of education, enlightenment, entertainment, and vocation.

I was forty when I moved to Williamsburg, three years older than Governor Jefferson when he left Williamsburg because the capital was moved to Richmond. Yet in midlife I was struck by the same sense of enlightenment that must have intrigued Jefferson when he first arrived at William and Mary. Though I had portrayed Jefferson for twelve years in Philadelphia, where there remain many well-preserved colonial buildings, Philadelphia did not offer the same all-encompassing ambience of the colonial world as may be found in Williamsburg.

I've gained a better understanding of Jefferson and his world by living within the Historic Area. Residing in a reconstructed eighteenth-century building in the midst of the comings and goings of this restored colonial town has enabled me to better understand the four-mile-an-hour world in which Jefferson lived and the close interactions he had in a city composed of many walks of life, including the enslaved. Living here highlights the modern conveniences, like air-conditioning, that Jefferson did without and inspires me to consider what that was like and how that might have affected him. Also, the manners of his day were vastly different from those of today, a profound realization when contemplating how Jefferson interacted socially and in business.

PART II
INTERPRETING

REHEARSING *and* IMPROVISING

I was led into interpreting the persona of Thomas Jefferson through the passion for history I developed in my childhood. I also came to this vocation through a love of theater. I can hardly recall a time growing up when I wasn't fascinated by and involved in theater—in school plays, neighborhood plays, and later semi-professional theater and finally as a professional actor, stage director, and producer.

When I began portraying Jefferson at Independence Hall, I instinctually applied both my history knowledge and my theater

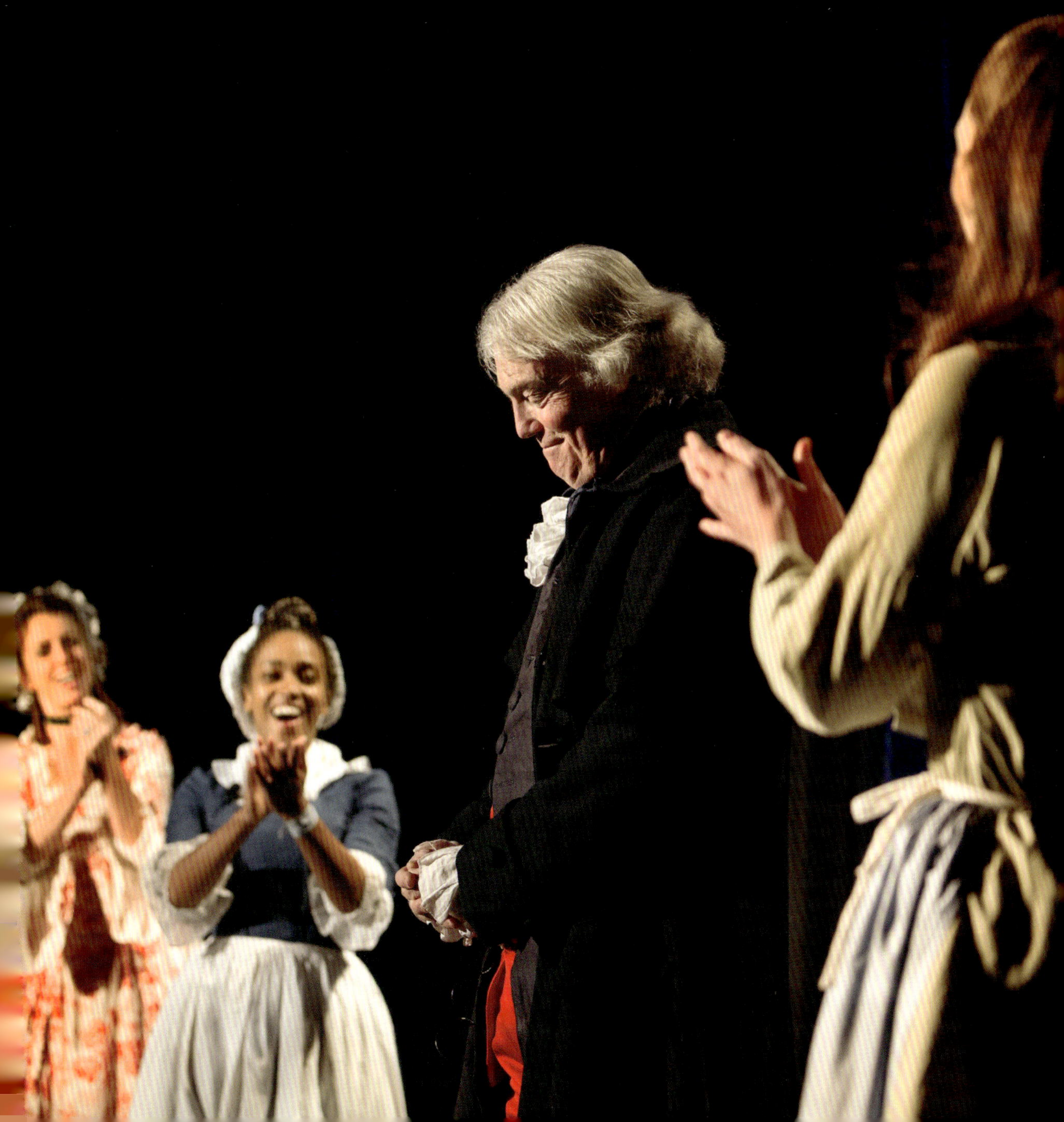

experience. I knew I had to be responsible for getting the history right. However, the theatrical element in the art of interpretation is the hook—helping people to suspend their disbelief so they may enter more easily into Jefferson's world.

This art does not improve overnight. It requires constant study, rehearsal, and interaction.

The costume certainly helps. Much debate continues over whether one can present historical interpretation out of costume. Without a question you can succeed out of costume. Our National Park Service and many successful historic sites accomplish this beautifully, focusing our interests and inspiring our hearts and imagination. But in the art of first-person historical interpretation, the costume is truly a first step toward suspending disbelief.

To successfully provoke imagination within historical context, one needs to rehearse, just as you rehearse a play. Had I been appearing as Thomas Jefferson five days a week in Philadelphia, that would have been the best preparation for day-to-day appearances in Williamsburg. However, in Philadelphia I appeared as Jefferson only sporadically. In the beginning, it was perhaps once every two or three months, and then within about a year it evolved into monthly appearances. At the time, I made a living performing in murder mysteries, industrials, voice-overs, books on tape, British music halls, Gilbert and Sullivan, the

Walnut Street Theatre, and community theaters in and around Philadelphia.

Within twenty-four hours of my arriving in Williamsburg, I was presenting upwards of three to four programs a day, five days a week. In between, I had to be "on" nearly constantly in the Historic Area. There was no rehearsing for the programs I presented during that summer of 1993. In fact, there was no time to rehearse. The rehearsals got rolled into the performances.

One of the merits of my hiring was that I already had more than a decade of experience. However, my work as Jefferson in Philadelphia had predominantly been limited to photo ops, celebrations, school visits, and appearing for tour groups at Independence Hall and the re-creation of the house in which Jefferson wrote the Declaration. In Williamsburg I was in character the entire day. The programs usually included twenty minutes of presentation and forty minutes of questions and answers.

Walking down Duke of Gloucester Street in costume, one is always at the behest of the public. Conversations in character may ensue at any moment, requiring you to create historical context to make those moments feel real and relevant today. This remains the foundation of historical interpretation. Only by living in the moment—a constant, spontaneous, impromptu, improvisational "rehearsal"—can the art of historical interpretation be mastered.

54

The information an interpreter brings to these improvisations springs not only from a sense of the traits of human nature but also from the research and understanding of the character and the times: manners, habits, customs, fashion, and language. The guest's curiosity drives the interaction, and the interpreter's skill sustains the first impression.

The guest often initiates the conversation: "Good day, Mr. Jefferson."

And I reply, "Good day, sir. How are you?" Or "Good day. May I be of assistance?"

"Where are you going, Mr. Jefferson?"

In the years when I portrayed the young, Revolutionary Jefferson, I might reply, "I am making my way to the Capitol. There are a number of burgesses gathering with the idea in mind to discuss the offenses of the Stamp Act. Have you read about that recently in the newspapers?"

And the conversation has begun.

Historical interpretation requires extended energy and stamina. One is called upon to create a living, breathing individual, to react spontaneously in split seconds to the moment in history, and to get the history right. Improvisation, the essence of historical interpretation, requires a secure knowledge of the facts as well as the historic person's particular—and peculiar—personal traits, frame of mind, and relevance to history. It can become a lifelong pursuit building the knowledge base and perfected presence of a historical character. The career of Hal Holbrook, as Mark Twain, is an example of the perfection of this art. Not only did Mr. Holbrook create scripted theatrical presentations, but some of his finest moments occurred when he went off script.

Unlike working on a book, working in historical interpretation is never-ending—it continues to live and breathe with every new performance. Interpreting is also unlike working solely as a scripted actor, where you rehearse your lines and then perform them at showtime.

As an interpreter, you are in front of the public day in, day out, sometimes seven days a week. You are not just memorizing and speaking history. In many ways, you actually live it.

SOURCES

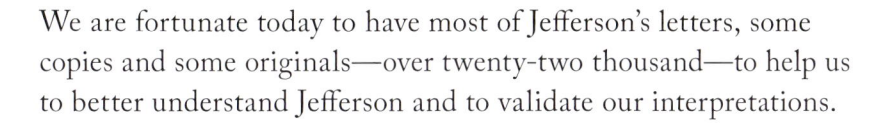

We are fortunate today to have most of Jefferson's letters, some copies and some originals—over twenty-two thousand—to help us to better understand Jefferson and to validate our interpretations.

During his retirement years, Jefferson began to cast an eye towards posterity when writing to lifelong friends such as John Adams, James Madison, James Monroe, Benjamin Rush, and Charles Willson Peale. He became more relaxed with his friends, wrote more about his feelings toward life, and reflected upon the remarkable history they were privileged to witness. In these letters of his autumn years, one reads more of his personality and glimpses more into his mind, manners, and morals.

Some years ago, Cary Carson, Colonial Williamsburg's vice president of Research at the time and a respected author and historian, was writing an article on Jefferson in Williamsburg and asked me to provide the source for Jefferson's statement that Williamsburg was the capital of good manners, hospitality, and education. I said, "No problem," believing it a simpler task than it turned out to be.

I thought the reference was a direct quote from one of Jefferson's later letters, but extensive research through his correspondence proved fruitless. I then turned to the work of the renowned Jefferson biographer Dumas Malone, who, over forty years, published the six-volume biography *Jefferson and His Time*. I did find the reference therein but only in an obscure footnote that nearly led to a dead end were it not for an unrelated footnote in the same biography that pointed to the Jefferson family papers at the University of Virginia. There, I discovered, in a manuscript at the Alderman Library, that Jefferson's grandson Thomas Jefferson Randolph had written that his grandfather referred to Williamsburg as the capital of good manners, the capital of hospitality, and the capital of education. I felt extremely honored and useful to know that in my craft of historical interpretation I could support my senior colleague's academic pursuits.

PART II: INTERPRETING

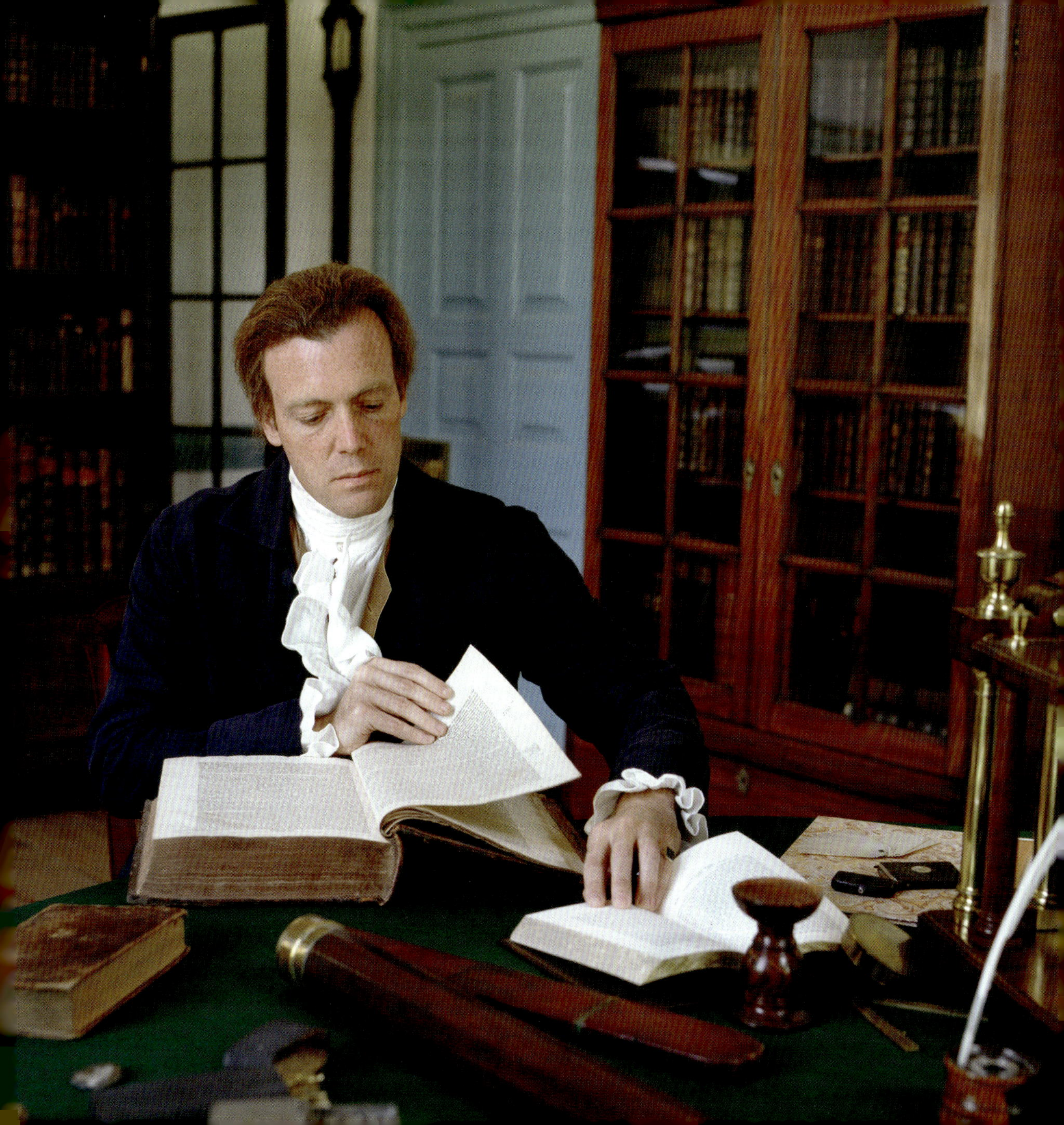

At Farmington, the Speed family home in Kentucky, in 1991, Barker points out Jefferson's floor plan for the house, on which the final plan may have been based.

In a curious way we are sometimes like the monks of the medieval world keeping alive the history of the ancient world, bringing to the surface what might otherwise be lost.

And, sometimes, in Jefferson's persona I have been prone to say things for which there may not be precise documentation. One must be cautious and not throw around fiction that overwhelms the facts, but at the same time you need to fill in the gaps where

PART II: INTERPRETING

there is no factual documentation in order to provide further historical context. For example, although we have no documentation for it, as Jefferson I often refer to Philadelphia as the northernmost southern city. The goal of a historical interpreter is to provoke and inspire, to bring people into the story, to make them feel the reality of the moment. You must connect with them to help them understand these were real living people, to help them think they are engaging not only with Thomas Jefferson but also with other persons of the past.

As much as possible, I use Jefferson's words. But I connect his words with my own—to tell a story, to paint a picture, to make a point. Jefferson's words are the meat, but there are a lot of sauces and condiments that can flavor that meat.

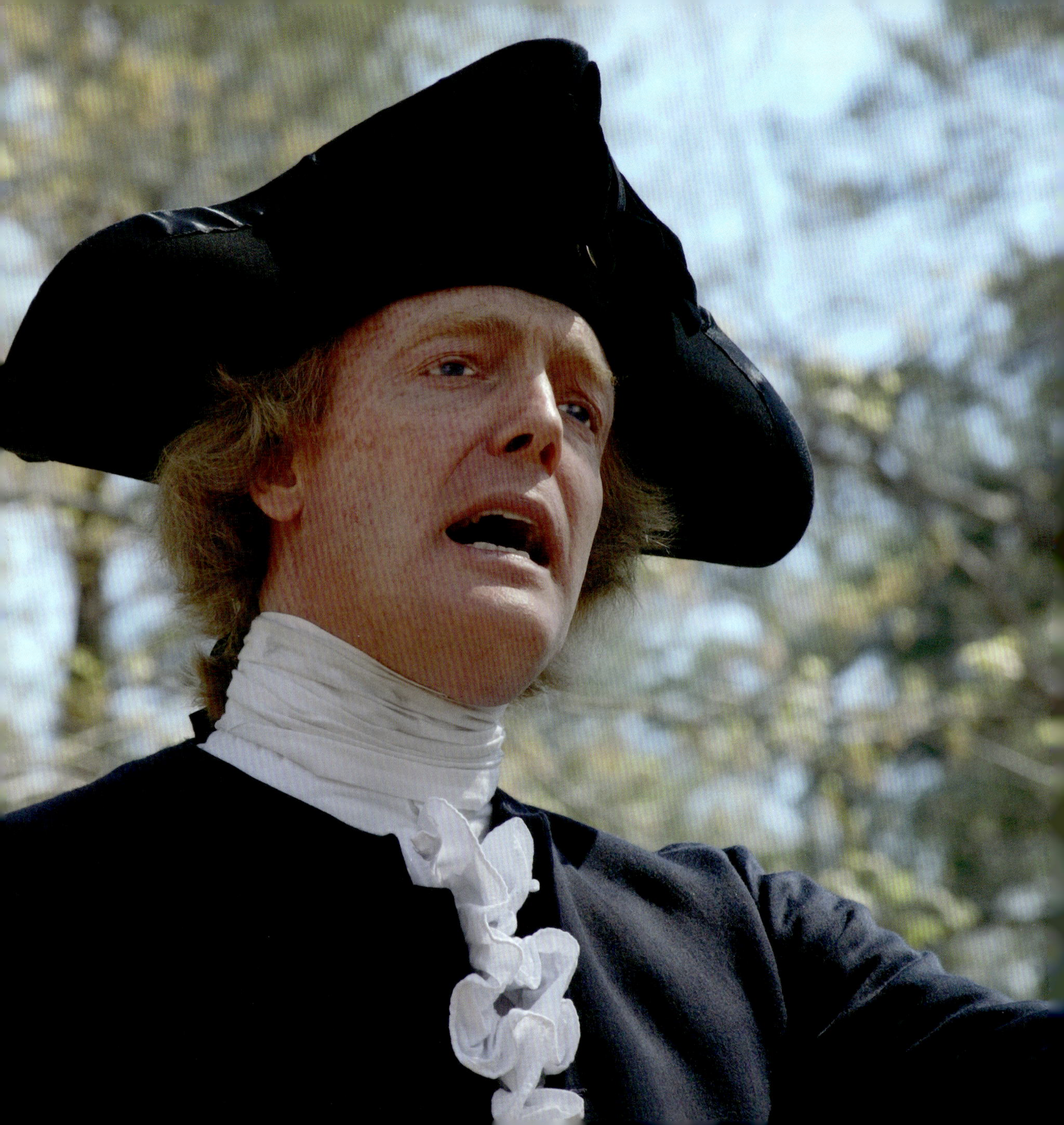

INTERPRETATION
and DIPLOMACY

Happily there are many occasions when a guest or a colleague has an extensive knowledge of Jefferson and enjoys reading his papers to gain a better understanding of him. It is then a distinct pleasure, in persona as Jefferson, to converse with them. These conversations can be quite lively and often delve deeply into a variety of topics.

There are also many occasions in which people approach me with their particular preconceived ideas of Jefferson. Sometimes these are grounded in fact, but for those who may be unfamiliar or confused in their opinions, I encourage them to read the primary sources and Jefferson's own words on a subject.

At times guests will take something out of context and harp on it despite the fact that Jefferson has written conclusively to the contrary. Then, too, my response is to refer to the original sources. In this era of "alternative facts" and "presentism" (approaching the past with a bias predicated on today's standards or sentiments), primary sources must remain our foundation. They remind us of the context of the times and are the only true foundation upon which we can build valid interpretations.

There is always an element of diplomacy in the interpretative method. If someone persists in disagreeing, there is really nothing one can do except to say, "With due respect, I welcome your opinion on the matter. How fortunate we are as Americans to be free to agree to disagree. A difference of opinion ought not be a difference of principle." This expression, in itself, is a Jeffersonian opinion as well as a principle that protects open and free debate.

Quite often, quoting Jefferson helps to inspire the recollection of hearing or reading the words before. Their application to current controversies can be extremely profound. Jefferson's first inaugural address remains a classic reminder of our nation's founding principles. On occasion, when I am approached in persona by guests who are upset with current politics, I quote from Jefferson's first

PART II: INTERPRETING

inaugural: "If there be any among us who would wish to dissolve this union or to change its republican form, let them stand undisturbed as monuments of the safety with which error of opinion may be tolerated where reason is left free to combat it."

Though not as often as some may think, guests are prone to pursue the controversy over Jefferson's relationship with Sally Hemings. The relationship has been speculated upon since it first appeared in an anti-Jefferson newspaper in 1802. It was used to jab at Jefferson politically. The controversy has continued even since DNA analysis in 1998. There has been much written on the subject, especially in the latter part of the last century. Of special importance is the work of Annette Gordon-Reed, beginning with her well-researched *Thomas Jefferson and Sally Hemings: An American Controversy* in 1997 and continuing with her Pulitzer Prize–winning *The Hemingses of Monticello: An American Family* in 2009.

The picture that Gordon-Reed paints should come as no surprise to students of history. Personally, I long ago recognized and continue to acknowledge the intimate relationships between black and white that have existed in America for centuries. To be true to a first-person portrayal of Thomas Jefferson, I have to treat the issue as he would. Historical primary sources remind us that Jefferson never publicly confirmed or denied these reports. He refused to lie about it but also refused to put his family or himself at risk. Thus, I answer questions about the Hemings family by saying, "Well, I am certainly aware of this national controversy. However, I have never made a public statement upon the matter. You ask that of me now, and yet I am concerned that we may put words into the mouth of history that were never spoken."

I also sometimes add (and always think) that I am concerned as well that Ms. Hemings is not here with us now to speak for herself. I ask people to consider: Are you asking me to speak for her? A sensitive, humane, and respectful recognition of Sally Hemings, her family, and the millions enslaved for life upon the "promised land" of American soil is long overdue. It is our obligation and responsibility to ensure that they never be forgotten and that they be remembered as equal to all others who helped build our nation.

In June 2018, Monticello unveiled a groundbreaking exhibit on Sally Hemings. In the intimate setting of one of the south wing chambers, Madison Hemings's oral history is combined with projected images—starting with plain black images on a white wall that evolve with color and movement. The effect is emotionally profound as the history of Mr. Jefferson's Monticello and his enslaved family takes on new life out of eyewitness accounts of voices long ignored.

With the enslaved Jupiter (portrayed by Richard Josey).

CONNECTING
with the AUDIENCE

Often a guest will simply ask, "Who are you?" or "Why are you dressed like that?"

I usually reply, "My name is Thomas Jefferson, and to whom do I have the pleasure of making this introduction?" This simple foil connects with the guest. From there I strive to sustain the conversation by connecting their interests with those of Jefferson.

A historical interpreter typically knows more about the period being interpreted than the general public. So the art of historical

Outside the Governor's Palace.

interpretation must be secured on a comfortable canvas of conversation where the guest and interpreter paint together those images and feelings they have in common.

As Thomas Jefferson, I may help the individual understand more clearly what is meant by "We hold these truths to be self-evident, that all men are created equal, that they are endowed by their Creator with certain unalienable rights, that among these are life, liberty and the pursuit of happiness." In these few select and powerful words, Jefferson captures a universal desire in human nature. We are not all born equal in abilities and talents, but we are all born equal under the laws of nature. However, we are born into the laws of man. And there the conflict—and a conversation—may begin.

The various venues for historical interpretation are always challenging. There's a difference interpreting in a coffeehouse setting or in a garden or a parlor as opposed to being on a formal stage and speaking to hundreds of people.

There is freedom to be more comfortable, intimate, and down-to-earth while speaking in a setting such as the Tucker House parlor. At the same time, one's "parlor manners" must come into play, never forgetting the manners of the historical period were vastly different from today. The bond with the guest begins with mutual respect. It may begin through acknowledging common experiences through the art of conversation, weaving one subject into the next, explaining how you arrived on horseback or carriage or maybe by walking from miles away. After all, guests have made their own way to Williamsburg by particular means as well.

The formal onstage appearance requires a more pronounced theatrical presentation. There needs to be more decisive stage blocking. A larger audience may be accommodated on benches in the Palace garden or in an amphitheater setting such as behind the Coffeehouse in the Historic Area. In these venues, the audience

▸ CONNECTING WITH THE AUDIENCE

expects a somewhat formal presentation, and you appear before them more as a public speaker. Still, the job of a historical interpreter remains to pull people into the living, breathing past and help them realize those moments were as alive as any today.

At the end of open-air presentations, I usually enjoy calling upon a young child from the audience and welcoming the child to join me onstage. I will then ask his or her name and introduce them to the audience. I tell the child that an argument has continued throughout history about what is the more powerful image to pass the torch of liberty from one generation to the next: "Is it the sword or the pen?"

Nine times out of ten, the "young citizen" will think about it but a moment and then reply, "The pen." Even should the child say the sword, I remind the child and the audience that Mr. Jefferson was commissioned a colonel of Virginia militia during the American Revolution and kept his sword of that rank throughout his entire life. He knew well that the sword must be drawn at times. I tell of the wisdom that can be written with the pen.
I then present to the child the gift of a quill pen and say, "With faith and hope, honor and gratitude, our history is now in your hands. You may wish to write down what happens this very day, and perhaps your own eyewitness account may someday be read by multitudes hundreds of years from now. In this way your history will remain alive by your pen."

With Katie Couric at the University of Virginia's Bicentennial Celebration.

In any conversation, whether public or private, there are interruptions. Live theater is no exception. I have been in many open-air conversations with guests when a helicopter flies over. Why ignore it? As is often said in theater, use it. I look up and say, "I declare! That is the largest dragonfly I have ever seen in my entire life. It certainly does refute the comte de Buffon's idea that the flora and fauna in America is inferior to anything found throughout the kingdoms of Europe." Such a diversion allows for an opportunity to speak of Buffon's thirty-six-volume *Histoire Naturelle*, published over a period of nearly forty years, 1749–1788, in which Buffon purported the denigrated condition of American

▸ CONNECTING WITH THE AUDIENCE

animal life due to what he said was the generally cold and wet climate of the American continent. I enjoy adding, "It's clear the comte de Buffon has never been to Virginia in summertime."

Or let's say you are engaged in a conversation when a child or even an adult says, "Wait a minute, you're dead. You're not really here."

I enjoy answering, "I beg your pardon. Can you read?"

He or she will of course say yes, and I will reply, "Then you are able to read what I have written?"

When they answer proudly yes, I remind them, "Then do I not remain alive? Words will always live and breathe through those who read them and encourage others to do the same."

In persona, I try to hold fast to "being" Thomas Jefferson. However, I try not to forget it is theater. Shakespeare made a valid point that may be applied to teaching history when he gave Hamlet the line, "The play's the thing" (wherein Hamlet will catch the conscience of the king and, by implication, historical interpreters can catch the conscience of their audience).

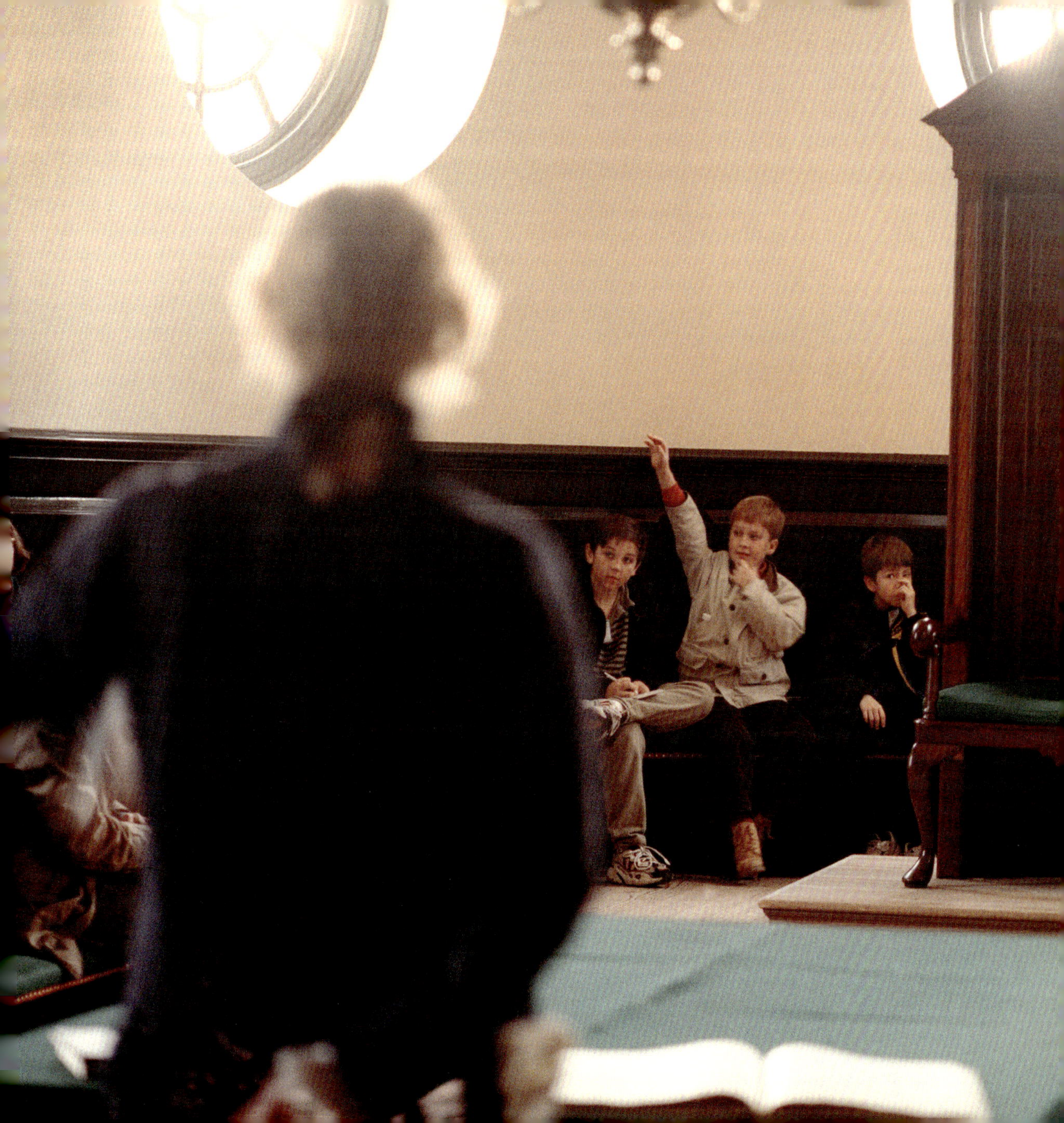

MAKING HISTORY RELEVANT

The essence of first-person historical interpretation is to relate the past as alive and breathing as it was however many years ago. That means helping people understand how the past continues to be relevant. In particular, historical interpretation can help to remind us of the principles of our American Revolution, principles that can still guide Americans today.

It is not the job of a historical interpreter to take a political stand. Yet the arguments of Jefferson's time are still the arguments we are having today—over religion, over race, over immigration, over the scope and power of government, over education, over business and corporate interests.

Over two centuries ago, Jefferson—and many others, famous and anonymous, men and women, free and enslaved—were grappling with the idea of America and what it means to be an American citizen. One thing was beginning to appear certain: we were becoming less British while becoming a distinct people unto ourselves. English law still prevailed, but regional, ethnic, and heretofore unknown social habits and customs amongst a growing diverse population were creating new legal challenges. Even before our U.S. Constitution was written, we were wondering: Who are "We the people"? We still are in conflict over this same question today.

In Jefferson's day "We the people" were defined as those who could vote and have a voice in our government. It did not mean all Americans living within our United States. It meant only white male freeholders twenty-one years of age and older. However, immigration, the settling of the west, and voting rights were always part of our national debate.

The job of a historical interpreter is to make the connections between past and present, to help people understand that the American experiment that began with the American Revolution continues today and into the future.

At the 2006 gubernatorial inauguration festivities in Williamsburg.

In persona as Jefferson, I have continued to express his opinions in his own words for nearly forty years regardless of political climate. Yet these words continue to be received differently depending on the political winds. I do not waver in expressing Jefferson's thoughts on religious freedom and the separation between church and state or on the dangers of an economy controlled by a self-professed aristocratic elite. I am always mindful to subjugate my own opinions to those of Jefferson's and to express his own unwavering opinions as he described them in his own writings. This sometimes offends some people, but it is necessary in order to maintain the integrity of historical interpretation.

One of the most influential writers on historical interpretation, especially at the National Park Service, was Freeman Tilden. As early as the 1940s, Tilden stressed the importance of remaining true to the mind and personality of a historical character. Tilden stressed the importance of engaging the visitor through questions, anecdotes, storytelling, and commentaries—all delivered with the vocabulary, manners, and customs of the period. Most importantly, he demanded the interpreter be familiar with the facts.

To make the past relevant today does not require coming out of historical character or the context of a previous time. After 9/11, I was often asked as Jefferson about the 2001 attacks on the World Trade towers and the Pentagon and the downing of United Airlines flight 93. A sensitive and respectful comment is always necessary when comparing a traumatic instance in our nation's modern history with anything that may be presumed similar in our past. In persona as Jefferson I remind people of the attacks by the Barbary pirates our forebears suffered in the colonial period and during the administrations of Presidents Washington, Adams, and Jefferson: "I believe I may understand the conflict to which you are referring. You mean the attacks of the Barbary pirates?" Then I discuss how we must stand strong against these pirates but caution that Jefferson's war against the kingdom of Tripoli in Africa is not a war against Muslims. It is a war to preserve "peace, commerce, and honest friendship with all nations, entangling alliances with none."

Even placing a current event in historical context must always be done with care, especially when the current event has been traumatic. History can provide valuable perspective, but interpreters cannot entirely assuage the pain people feel.

Representing the three branches of government established by the Constitution: Congressman Thaddeus Stevens (portrayed by Bill Weldon), Chief Justice John Marshall (D. Cash Arehart), and the sliding President Jefferson.

TALKING *to* KIDS

Good advice for any interpreter is not to speak down to children. They are more receptive and engaged when you speak with them as you would adults. When I was a child, a popular television show was Art Linkletter's *Kids Say the Darndest Things*. Linkletter never spoke down to children, and they thus felt more at ease with him. Mr. Rogers had the same gift. The result is often wonderfully whimsical and provocative. It also can be profound.

I remember a presentation when a little girl raised her hand and asked, "Mr. Jefferson, what did you do with your tomatoes?"

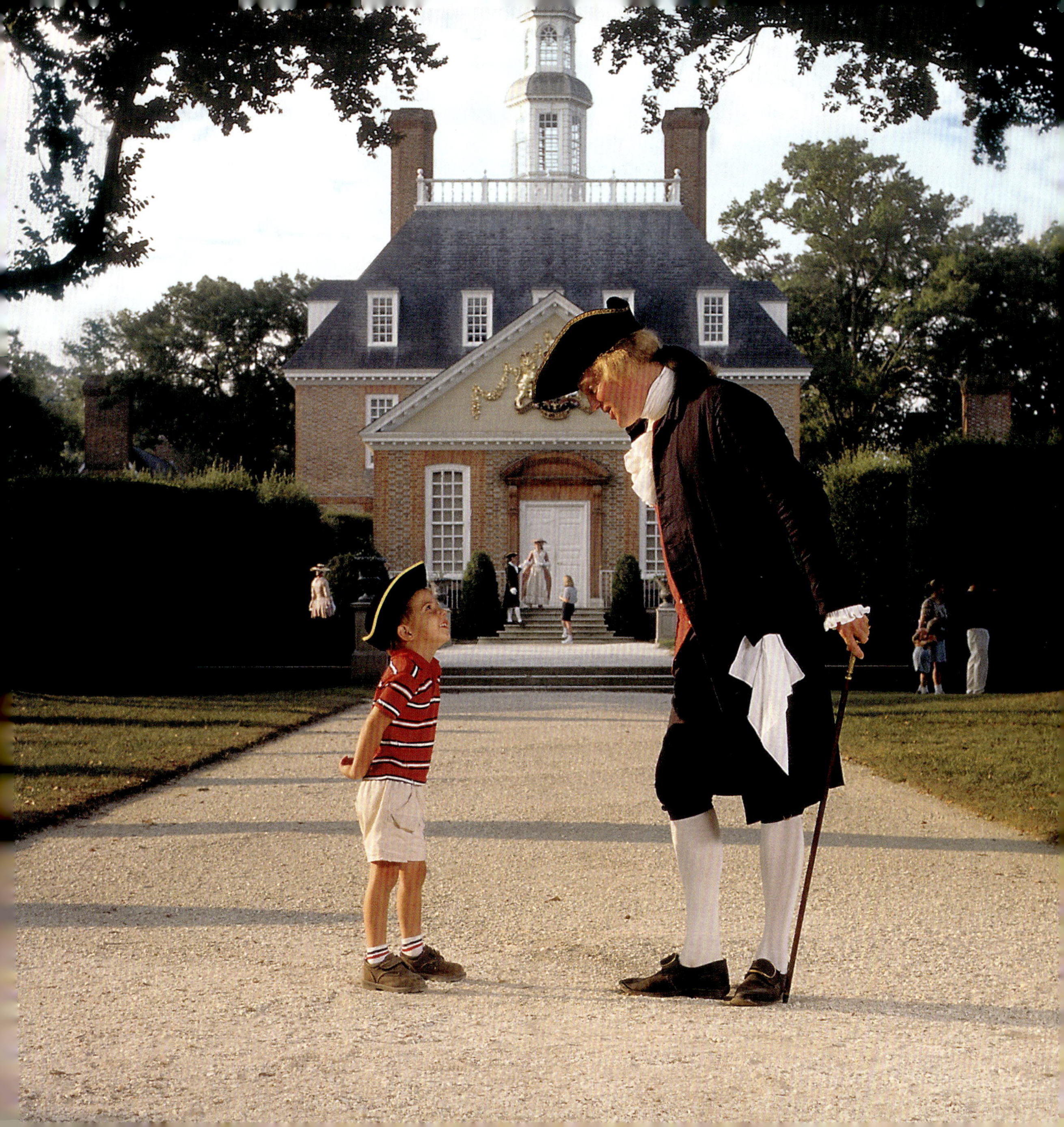

With Patrick Henry (portrayed by Richard Schumann) and the Reverend Gowan Pamphlet (James Ingram).

She was so sincere, so interested and serious. I smiled and said, "What do you know about my interest in tomatoes?"

She said, "Well, I know that many people didn't like them, but you liked them and enjoyed growing them."

I happily replied to her, "You're absolutely right. Many people would not even allow themselves the pleasure to taste a tomato. Do you know why? They thought the tomato was poisonous because it is part of a family of vegetables that includes a poisonous vegetable referred to as the deadly nightshade. Now, I do not suggest cooking up the deadly nightshade, but other vegetables in that same family, like the tomato, are safe and healthy—and even delicious."

The two of us launched into a delightful conversation about Jefferson's promotion of tomatoes, and the audience seemed to thoroughly enjoy learning about the eighteenth-century superstition about eating tomatoes.

On a more profound note, I'll never forget the little girl who came up to "Mr. Jefferson" and tugged on my coattail while I was speaking with others. I turned to her, bending down to her height, and she asked, "Mr. Jefferson, what do you tell your older brother who is going off to war and is very worried that he might not come home?" This was during the time of the Iraq War, and you could have heard a pin drop amongst the silenced gathering.

Jefferson may have been approached by children asking the same question when he sent troops to fight piracy in Tripoli or when he was governor of Virginia during the Revolutionary War.

I knelt down to her and said, "Dear, tell your brother that you're going to write to him and, most of all, that you want letters from him. Tell him that he is helping to make you and your family safe and free and that you feel happy and secure and comforted by what he is going to do. Let him know that you and your family are with him in his heart as he remains with you all in your hearts. Let him know how proud you all are that he's helping to defend our nation and what an honor it is to have him as your brother."

In Market Square Tavern.

TEACHING TEACHERS

Colonial Williamsburg's Teacher Institute programming is a wonderful opportunity to help open the eyes of teachers who in turn are influencing youth and their futures across the country. Whenever I interact with teachers, I encourage them to encourage their students to read the primary documents and sources. I suggest they look at a provocative sentence in one of Jefferson's letters or public papers in the context of the rest of the source and the history of the time.

Colonial Williamsburg has always been involved with outreach programs in the neighborhoods immediately around the Historic Area. But, beginning with our donor societies created in the 1970s and our Colonial Williamsburg Teacher Institute founded in 1989, the Foundation has supported extensive outreach across the nation to introduce the Colonial Williamsburg experience.

Since 1996 I have had the delightful opportunity to travel to California each year to help kick off the Teacher Institute programs for teachers who will be coming to Williamsburg for the immersion experience in the summer. Through the Teacher Institute, teachers across the country are provided with techniques to take the history of the founding of our nation into their classrooms. The Institute was initiated by dedicated supporters of John D. Rockefeller Jr.'s dream to restore the former colonial capital of Virginia so that the future may learn from the past.

For over twenty years I have traveled as "Mr. Jefferson" throughout the country. I have been fortunate to perform as Mr. Jefferson in nearly every state in our nation. When I hear people complain about big government, a complaint to which Jefferson was certainly sympathetic, I respond in persona by remarking how extraordinary it is that we have now grown to nineteen states!

MR. PRESIDENT

In persona as Jefferson, I am often asked: Did you want to be president? Did you enjoy being president? For years, in character as the younger image of Jefferson, I would react rather startled that such a farfetched and lofty future would be my lot.

When I was interpreting the young Jefferson in Williamsburg, this was an especially challenging question because I was portraying Jefferson before he became president. When he first arrived in Williamsburg at the age of sixteen, he had no idea that in another ten years he would be seated as a burgess in the Virginia

Examining the jawbone of an elk collected during the Lewis and Clark expedition. **OPPOSITE** *Discussing the Lewis and Clark expedition with Meriwether Lewis (portrayed by Willie Balderson).*

At the John F. Kennedy Presidential Library and Museum in Boston.

House of Burgesses. He had no idea then that in ten years he would become the second elected governor of the new commonwealth of Virginia any more than he knew he would be the last resident of the Governor's Palace. As governor, he never thought that in three years he would sail to France and return five years later to take on the office of the first secretary of state under our new national Constitution. Would it have occurred to him that he would be invited to stand for the office of president in 1796 and then again in 1800? Each of us may ponder these same questions with respect to the vagaries of our own lives and futures.

Between 1776 and 1789, if Jefferson had any ambition to be president of the Continental Congress or of Congress under the Articles of Confederation, neither he nor his contemporaries ever wrote about it. However, there is evidence of an interest to be president of the United States in his correspondence during the period he was retired from the office of secretary of state, 1794–1796, and during his term as vice president, 1797–1801. Through these seven years, the Anti-Federalists, with Jefferson and Madison as their philosophical leaders, were engaged in efforts to thwart Alexander Hamilton's plans for a strong central government and national financial system. As a consequence, Jefferson was invited to stand for the office of president and to oppose his friend and former collaborator on the committee to draft our Declaration of Independence, John Adams. But all this occurred more than a decade after his time in Williamsburg.

With John Adams (portrayed by Sam Goodyear) and Abigail Adams (Abigail Schumann) in Howard Ginsberg's play Jefferson & Adams.

As for Bill Barker, did I have any idea when I came to Williamsburg in 1993 to portray the young Thomas Jefferson, the Revolutionary Thomas Jefferson, the member of the Virginia House of Burgesses, the immediate former student of the College of William and Mary, the immediate former student of George Wythe, that in two decades I would be called upon in day-to-day

PART II: INTERPRETING

programming and appearances to interpret Thomas Jefferson as president? I had no more of an idea that would be asked of me than Thomas Jefferson had an idea he would stand for the presidency.

Perhaps there was something of an omen early on in my employment at Colonial Williamsburg that, should I stay on, the persona of President Jefferson could evolve quite naturally. Within three years of my arrival, Colonial Williamsburg created a program in 1996 titled "The Campaign of '96." It interpreted the first presidential election after President Washington retired. We presented the program at the old Williamsburg movie theater, shortly before its renovation to become the Kimball Theatre. At the time I was called upon to create the program, I was forty-three, thirteen years younger than Jefferson when he first stood for the presidency. Jefferson came in second to Federalist John Adams, with the result that Adams was president and Jefferson, the Anti-Federalist and runner-up, was vice president—the first time that the two top offices were filled by persons from opposing parties.

INTERPRETERS
of the FUTURE

Just as important as Colonial Williamsburg's devotion to maintaining our historical buildings is the Foundation's dedication to sustaining our interpretive history. George Washington, Patrick Henry, Thomas Jefferson, James Madison, the enslaved preacher Gowan Pamphlet, the free woman of color Edith Cumbo, the schoolteacher Ann Wager, the enslaved double agent James Armistead Lafayette, the *Virginia Gazette* printer Clementina Rind, our foreign hero General Lafayette: these and others who populated eighteenth-century Williamsburg must continue to appear in persona to breathe life into our historic city.

With young Jefferson (portrayed by Kurt Smith) near the George Wythe House.

The Baptist preacher Gowan Pamphlet is interpreted by James Ingram and, as a younger man, by Joseph Feaster.

As I have grown older, well beyond the age of thirty-seven, when Jefferson as governor moved the capital of Virginia from Williamsburg to Richmond, it has become increasingly obvious that a younger persona of Jefferson would be more relevant and believable appearing in the colonial setting. I welcomed the idea of helping to audition a "young Jefferson," and Colonial Williamsburg could not have been more fortunate in discovering Kurt Smith. Kurt's presence ensures we can continue helping our young citizens to better understand our American story.

PART II: INTERPRETING

Mr. Jefferson mentored many bright souls to take on the responsibility of fulfilling the American promise. In mentoring Kurt, I have gained a greater understanding of Jefferson the mentor.

It has been and continues to be a symbiotic relationship. How many of us would have been grateful for someone to have told our younger selves, "Hey, watch out for this," or "Beware of that"? How many of us would welcome the feeling of rejuvenation by seeing a younger self? What a joy to, in some sense, set out boldly upon life's pathway once again—to relive all the wonderful hopes, aspirations, character building, and young friendships.

When Kurt and I first met, I assured him, "I'm not going to tell you what to say. Your own interpretation must be in your particular manner." But I could and did point him in the direction of valid resources and primary documents that provide Jefferson's opinions on nearly every subject under the sun. I seek to inspire him to understand the great responsibility to get Jefferson right. Our job is not to take a political stand. Our job is to make sure the history is as accurate as possible.

Kurt and I created a program called "Looking Forward, Looking Back," which we both enjoy. It is a meeting and a conversation between the older Jefferson and the younger persona. The older Jefferson is at first cautious but then realizes that the spirit of the younger Jefferson continues to inspire him.

Jefferson wrote to James Madison in September 1789, "The earth belongs always to the living generation," and he wrote to John Adams in August 1816, "I like the dreams of the future better than the history of the past." Working together, Kurt and I have gained a mutual appreciation about the future of Jefferson interpretation.

For example, Kurt says he does not want to sugarcoat Jefferson, and that has helped me make sure I do not conceal Jefferson's flaws. In return, I remind Kurt that he is in persona as Jefferson and must represent him as Jefferson represented himself, without apologies for positions that today seem unviable.

101

BECOMING JEFFERSON, BEING MYSELF

When people learn that I've been interpreting Jefferson for so long—for nearly forty years—they sometimes ask: Do you still know who *you* are? Are you able to take off your costume and be comfortable with yourself?

I have no doubt that Jefferson has become a part of my personal frame of mind, just as anyone's livelihood may become a part of them. But happily, I can still wear jeans and a T-shirt or coat and tie and feel comfortable as Bill Barker and not Thomas Jefferson. Putting on a persona and creating historical scenarios has been a

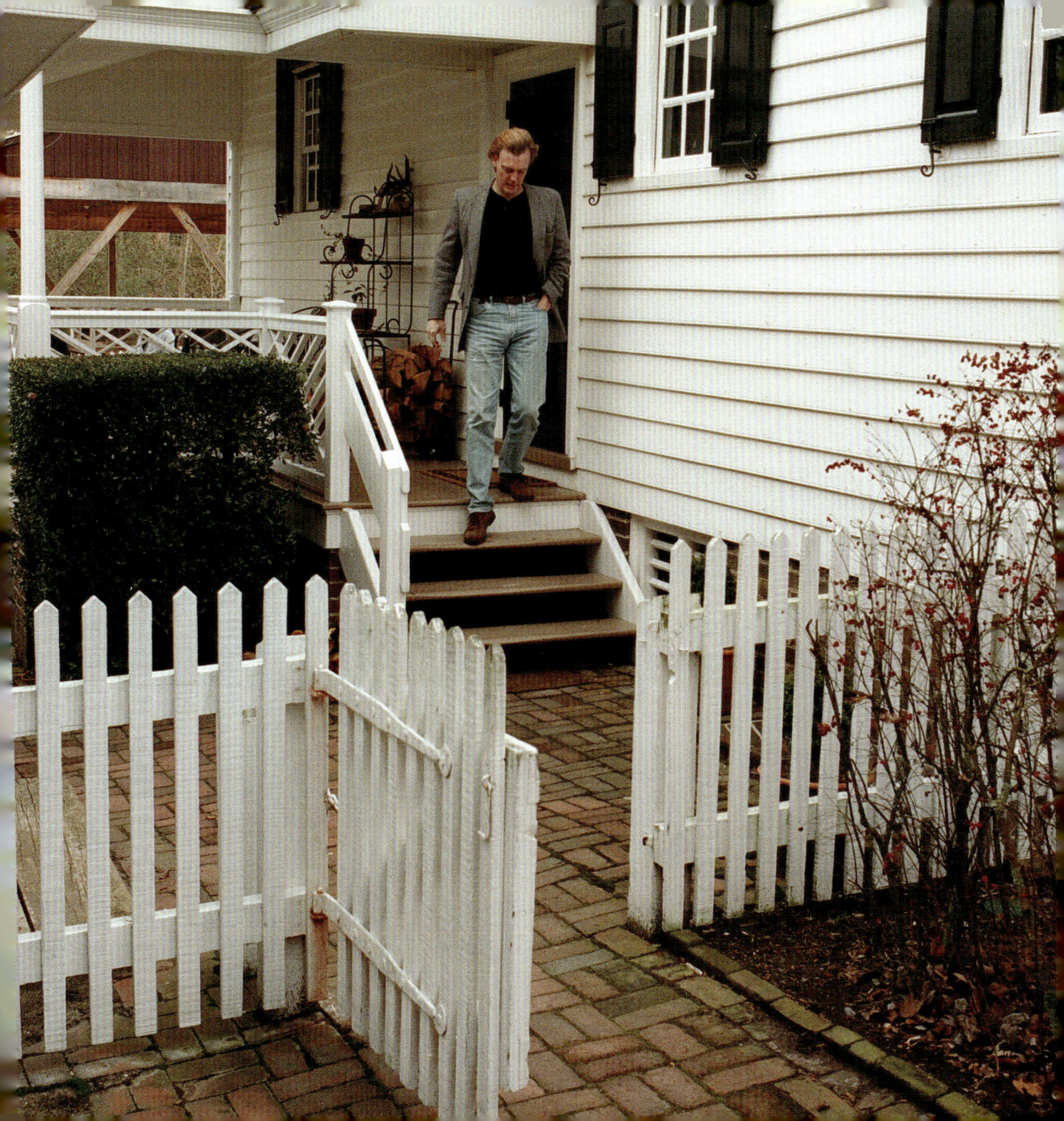

wonderful livelihood in which time can become a plateau and everything is happening at once, as Sir Francis Bacon suggested in his essay "The Vicissitude of Things." However, I remain the most content with who I am and with the times in which I am blessed to be living. Any era may always be "the best of times" and "the worst of times," as Charles Dickens wrote in the first line of *A Tale of Two Cities*. I am more than happy to be living in the greater health and general pursuit of happiness in these times.

People ask if I've grown into thinking like Jefferson. To which I answer immediately that I am decidedly not of his genius of intellect! Some presume that I might know all there is to know about him. Quite the contrary. Even his foremost biographer, Dumas Malone, after studying him and writing about him for the majority of his life, said that no one will ever truly know Thomas Jefferson entirely because the essence of who he really was remains elusive. Jefferson wanted it that way. He was a great proponent of personal privacy. In this respect, I am very much like him.

None of this implies that one cannot gain at least a friendly familiarity with Mr. Jefferson. Without question, Jefferson has become a good friend, and I have gained a sense of how Jefferson would think and feel when I read the newspapers, when I turn on the television, and when I hear commentary and conversations about current events. A wonderful aspect about Jefferson's sensibilities is that they are still so relevant to what we are thinking

105

and saying today. Clay Jenkinson of the weekly NPR radio program *The Thomas Jefferson Hour* is a valid source for how Jefferson might think about our concerns today. Jefferson had a remarkable capacity to relate to all time, which I think grew out of his own fascination with history. He was so well-read, especially in ancient history, and this provided for him the understanding of the past that inspired the vision he had for the future.

I do not always agree with what Mr. Jefferson thought and wrote. He was caught in the habits, customs, laws, and tastes of his own time. Though he had wonderful vision, he could not possibly see everything that would later transpire—any more than we can in our own time. We have the advantage in commenting about history because, in general, we know what happened. But we must always pause and reflect upon that advantage and humble ourselves. They knew no more of what would happen the next day in their time than we can know today what will happen tomorrow. Imagine what people are going to say about us two hundred years from now!

PART III

LEGACIES

GARDENS

I was born and brought up in the suburbs of Philadelphia. I have always had an appreciation for gardening and an appreciation of woods. Growing up, I was outdoors more than I was indoors. My father's family, originally from Virginia and later in North Carolina, were farmers for ten generations before I was born. I have a deep connection to the land. When I visited Monticello for the very first time, I instinctively felt that the cultivation of the soil was in my blood as it had been for Jefferson. Thomas Jefferson often referred to himself as "a savage of the mountains."

Behind the Governor's Palace.

In Philadelphia, I never had the opportunity to portray Jefferson as a gardener. I did portray him several times at Bartram's Garden, the colonial home of the botanists William and John Bartram, on the banks of the Schuylkill River near Philadelphia. However, I was usually there for cocktail receptions and social gatherings.

I have also long been familiar with the world-class Longwood Gardens in Pennsylvania. The initial arboretum was created in the eighteenth century by the Peirce brothers, with whom Jefferson was acquainted. Jefferson also knew the forebears of Pierre Samuel du Pont, who purchased the Peirce land in the early 1900s and created the magnificent gardens.

One of my first programs with Colonial Williamsburg was "Mr. Jefferson's Garden Walk," which was designed to reveal not only Jefferson's love of botany and horticulture but also his interest in landscape design. Creating the garden tour allowed me to acquaint myself with the beauty and evolution of garden design as seen in the Palace gardens.

Jefferson was familiar with the Governor's Palace gardens and the gardens in and about Williamsburg from the time he was a young man. He knew the celebrated Custis garden at the southeast corner of Francis and Nassau Streets, visited by William and John Bartram and inherited by Mrs. Washington's first husband, Daniel Parke Custis.

PART III: LEGACIES

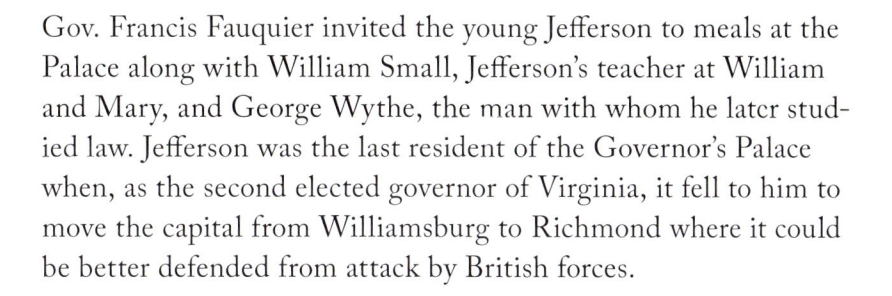

Gov. Francis Fauquier invited the young Jefferson to meals at the Palace along with William Small, Jefferson's teacher at William and Mary, and George Wythe, the man with whom he later studied law. Jefferson was the last resident of the Governor's Palace when, as the second elected governor of Virginia, it fell to him to move the capital from Williamsburg to Richmond where it could be better defended from attack by British forces.

Jefferson understood the evolution of the garden design at the Governor's Palace. He knew the garden had originally been planned by Alexander Spotswood during the first fifteen years of the eighteenth century. He knew the original was a walled-in,

▸ GARDENS

confined garden that was part of a tradition prevalent from the Middle Ages through the early eighteenth century. He recognized its evolution in design through its further expansion as the north wall was knocked down. Through successive administrations the garden's design likely evolved along more natural lines as England's did. The Palace gardens must have had some influence in Jefferson's early landscape designs of Monticello.

Jefferson was deeply interested in plants, those indigenous to Virginia and throughout the world. He wrote in his "Summary of Public Service," September 1800, "The greatest service which can be rendered any country is to add an useful plant to its culture, especially a bread grain." He did so in abundance at Monticello. He understood the value of plants for the table and for medicinal purposes, let alone for sheer beauty. The digitalis, or foxglove, is a good example of a very pretty flower that also has medicinal uses. This, too, he may have first seen in Williamsburg and particularly in the Palace gardens.

For fifteen years, I did the hour-long "Mr. Jefferson's Garden Walk." I always enjoyed drawing it to a close with Jefferson's own words, which he wrote in a letter to Charles Willson Peale in August 1811: "Tho' an old man, I am but a young gardener."

WINE

My parents were not teetotalers, but they were sparing with their drink. So my knowledge of wine was limited when I began my interpretation of Thomas Jefferson. As Jefferson wrote to James Madison in September 1785, "You see I am an enthusiast on the subject of the arts. But it is an enthusiasm of which I am not ashamed, as its object is to improve the taste of my countrymen, to increase their reputation, to reconcile to them the respect of the world and procure them its praise."

To Jefferson, viticulture was no less a study in fine art.

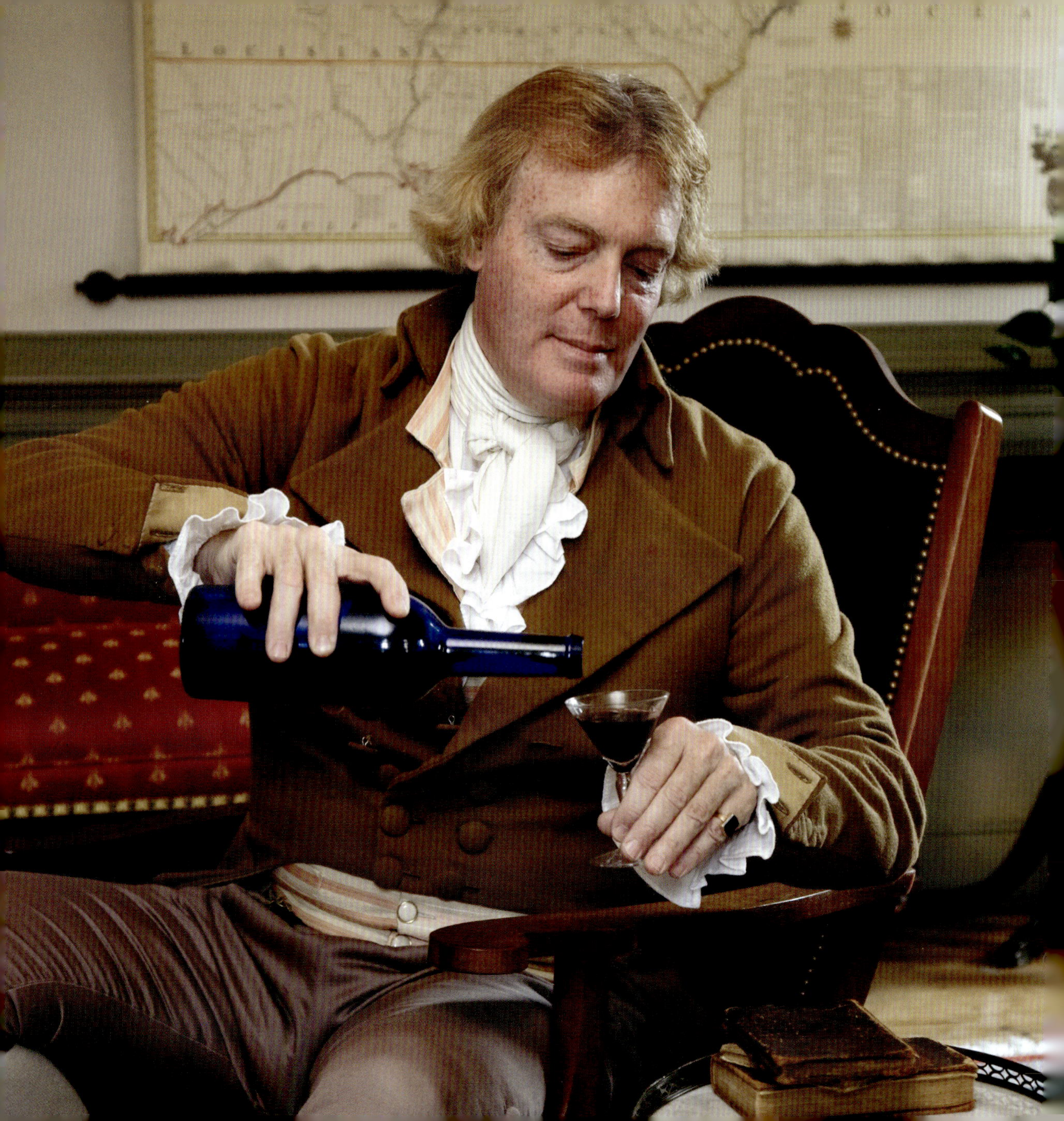
LOUISIANA

In his correspondence he wrote:

"Wine from long habit has become an indispensable for my health."

"We could, in the United States, make as great a variety of wines as are made in Europe: not exactly of the same kinds, but doubtless as good."

"No nation is drunken where wine is cheap, and none sober where the dearness of wine substitutes ardent spirits as the common beverage."

"I have lived temperately, eating little animal food, and that not as an aliment so much as a condiment for the vegetables, which constitute my principal diet. I double however the doctor's glass and a half of wine, and even treble it with a friend."

As a young man in Williamsburg, Jefferson was mostly familiar with heavy Madeiras, ports, and sherry, the fortified wines imported by Great Britain. Jefferson began his lifelong interest in the delicate art of viticulture when he served as minister plenipotentiary of our nation to France from 1785–1789. In his travels throughout Burgundy and then in and around Bordeaux, he became quite the accomplished connoisseur. Benjamin Franklin helped to familiarize his successor as ambassador to France with the finest wines of the kingdom when Jefferson first arrived in the late summer of 1784. They were then, as they are now, Meursault, Montrachet, Volnay, and Clos de Vougeot in Burgundy and Margaux, Lafite, Latour, Haut-Brion, and, of the Sauternes, Château d'Yquem in Bordeaux.

As a young student at William and Mary when Jefferson was invited to Governor Fauquier's table at the Governor's Palace, I can imagine that he experienced an elegantly set table, a French meal, and perhaps French wine. Francis Fauquier's family were French expatriates.

In Williamsburg—still a capital of hospitality, as Jefferson referred to it—I have nurtured a better understanding of Jefferson's love of wine. I have long been familiar with the indigenous vines in Virginia and in North America, specifically the muscat or muscadine grape, Tokay, fox grape, scuppernong, and concord grapes, and Colonial Williamsburg's extensive foodways and superb wine selection have helped to educate me on viticulture and foreign wine.

Colonial Williamsburg commenced its Cultural Expeditions programming in 1994 with its Raleigh Tavern Society trip to England. Our Jefferson tours to France began in 1995. On these trips, I learned more about what Jefferson was privileged to discover about French viticulture when he was in France. It was

PART III: LEGACIES

an incredible experience to walk through the actual vineyards in France where Jefferson visited. In these vineyards one has the opportunity to enjoy the same art of wine making that made Jefferson a lifelong devotee. Like Jefferson, I remain partial to the finest French wines.

During a 1999 visit to France, our group attended a reception hosted by the president of Burgundy, and of course a prominent subject of conversation was wine. One of our donors asked about a cache of bottles of wine that supposedly had been walled up in the

▸ WINE

basement of a town house in Paris from the time of the French Revolution. The bottles had Jefferson's initials etched on them.

The president of Burgundy looked at us smiling and said, "Oui, we have heard of this tall tale. How do we know these were Mr. Jefferson's bottles? We have never known anyone to take the time to etch their names or initials on their bottles. Would Mr. Jefferson have done that?"

Finally, he said simply, "Untrue. No Frenchman believes it. Nor should anyone believe it. Besides, it is but vinegar now anyway."

There has since been a book written titled *The Billionaire's Vinegar* that shows it was indeed all a ruse. The French already knew better.

As a consequence of better understanding Jefferson's love of viticulture and its importance in our national culture, the Jefferson wine dinners began in 1996. Colonial Williamsburg also has offered wine seminars at the Williamsburg Inn. These events have included many of the wines enjoyed by Jefferson as well as the increasing number of fine wines cultivated throughout Virginia and across our nation.

MILITIA

Hardly anyone thinks of Thomas Jefferson as a military man. His father, Peter Jefferson, was a colonel of Virginia militia. His father's father, whom he never knew, was Col. Thomas Jefferson the Younger. His great-grandfather was Col. Thomas Jefferson the Elder, also of Virginia militia. Jefferson was brought up understanding the need for militias to protect person and property, particularly on the frontier.

As the eldest son, Jefferson inherited the majority of his father's property along with a militia commission. He was commissioned as lieutenant of the Albemarle County militia in his late twenties, and in a few years, just as the American Revolution began, he received the commission as colonel of the same militia.

Jefferson was part of the militia even before he was elected to the House of Burgesses, even before he became an attorney. As a member of the Virginia House of Delegates, as a delegate of Virginia to the Continental Congress, as the second governor of Virginia, through all his years of public service, he retained his commissions of military rank.

As governor of the Commonwealth of Virginia, he considered it necessary to move the capital of Virginia from Williamsburg to Richmond in 1780 for military reasons. He knew Williamsburg was susceptible to enemy attack. Eventually, the British did invade Virginia, in January 1781, and occupied Williamsburg that summer. But by January 1781, Virginia's capital had been established at Richmond. Though Richmond was better defended, the government still had to retreat with the advance of the enemy in the spring of 1781. It found sanctuary in Charlottesville.

The tale of the midnight ride of Jack Jouett, Virginia's Paul Revere, is a worthy fact of Virginia history that ought never to be forgotten. On Monday morning, June 4, 1781—ironically the birthday of King George III and the day appointed to elect the third governor of the Commonwealth of Virginia—Jefferson was

Jack Jouett (portrayed by Stuart Lilie) rode to Monticello to warn Jefferson that the British were coming.

PART III: LEGACIES

seated at the breakfast table at Monticello with his personal secretary William Short and the gentleman who would be the third elected governor of Virginia, Gen. Thomas Nelson, also a signer of the Declaration of Independence. They were suddenly interrupted by the young Virginia militia captain Jack Jouett. The evening before, in his father's tavern in Cuckoo, Virginia, Jouett had overheard Lt. Col. Banastre Tarleton's officers discussing their plans to capture members of the Virginia House of Delegates meeting in Charlottesville and, in particular, Governor Jefferson.

Jouett rode all night through more than forty miles of dense Virginia forest to inform the governor of Tarleton's plans. With Jouett's warning Jefferson had time to prepare his family to retreat from Monticello and to warn the Virginia House of Delegates in Charlottesville. Then, as he noted, with his sword by his side Jefferson mounted his horse and rode across the valley of the Rivanna to an opposite mountaintop. There, he dismounted and knelt down to look through his spyglass to see whether Tarleton's troops, led by Capt. Kenneth McLeod, had ascended Monticello. His sword got in the way, so he unhooked it and placed it on the ground next to him. Through his glass he did not see any of McLeod's green-coated dragoons, so he prepared to ride back to Monticello, thankful that he had escaped the enemy attack. He rode but a few paces before realizing he had left his sword behind, so he rode back, dismounted, went to pick up the sword, and now saw smoke billowing over Monticello. He brought up his glass again and saw that his mountaintop was swarming with British dragoons. Jefferson's sword saved his life—without ever being unsheathed.

Incidentally, the Cuckoo Tavern, in Cuckoo, Virginia, was so named because of an elaborate cuckoo clock that had been carved by one of the Hessian prisoners of war who had been held in barracks in Charlottesville along what is still known as Barracks Road. Jefferson's civil treatment of those prisoners turned out to save Monticello. Tarleton's dragoons set fire to his tobacco crops and his barns and slaughtered his livestock, but they never

PART III: LEGACIES

touched the mansion house, which at the time housed all the records and archives of colonial Virginia. Jefferson had personally removed the documents from the secretary's office in Williamsburg. He felt their protection was assured so far west in the wilderness of Virginia.

Some accused Jefferson of cowardice for apparently fleeing Monticello in the face of the enemy. The Virginia House of Delegates set up a review commission to scrutinize Jefferson's actions during his last several days as governor. It found that in fact Jefferson did not flee but continued to serve as governor of Virginia for three days after Jouett's ride until Nelson could be elected the next governor. Michael Kranish clarified this legendary misunderstanding of Jefferson's last days as governor in his exceptional 2010 history *Flight from Monticello.* Kranish's book has proven to be a great resource for my first-person replies to the question of Governor Jefferson's cowardice.

Jefferson was never involved in, nor witnessed, any battles during the American Revolution, not even a skirmish. However, one of his very first actions as president of the United States was to declare war, with the consent of Congress, on the kingdom of Tripoli. This war against the Barbary pirates became known as Mr. Jefferson's War. It resulted in a U.S. victory after four and a half years, particularly as a result of the success of our marines on the shores of Tripoli.

Every Presidents' Day weekend, Colonial Williamsburg's George Washington, James Madison, and Thomas Jefferson all partake in an afternoon ceremony during which the three of us are honored to command and to fire cannon. Washington is of course well-known as a successful military leader, and Madison was president during the War of 1812 and even took to the field alongside Maryland troops during the British invasion of Washington, D.C., in August 1814. I portray President Jefferson wearing not only a sword but also a re-creation of his greatcoat, the original of which is owned by the Huntington Library in California. Jefferson's sword cannot always be seen underneath the greatcoat; I like to think of that as a metaphor for the hidden nature of his military side.

THE WHITE HOUSE

In the more than thirty-five years I've been impersonating our nation's third president, I have been privileged to be invited to "the President's House" several times. The first occasions, during the George H. W. Bush administration in the late 1980s, were the annual Fourth of July and Easter Egg Roll parties that took place on the South Lawn. These appearances continued intermittently through the Bill Clinton, George W. Bush, and Barack Obama administrations. In the autumn of 1992, I was invited to portray President Jefferson for ceremonies celebrating the two-hundredth anniversary of the building of the White House. These

The Rushmore presidents: George Washington (portrayed by Dean Malissa), Jefferson, Theodore Roosevelt (Gib Young), and Abraham Lincoln (Fritz Klein).

ceremonies took place at the White House and the Kennedy Center, also in Washington, D.C.

In April 2001, soon after the heated presidential election of 2000, newly inaugurated George W. Bush hosted a Thomas Jefferson birthday celebration and invited many Jefferson descendants, biographers, and historic site administrators to a day of speeches and an elegant buffet at the White House. I was invited to provide a first-person portrayal of President Jefferson before President Bush and the gathering in the East Room. I quoted Jefferson's first inaugural address: "Every difference of opinion is not a difference of principle.... We are all Republicans, we are all Federalists."

I then added my own comment upon the close results of the electoral vote: "May it please this gathering to learn my particular political platform has recently been recognized with the label 'Democratic-Republicans.'" Jefferson's party had become known as such in the electoral tie vote of the presidential election of 1800—exactly two hundred years before!

For Halloween 2016 I was invited to the White House along with fellow interpreters of the Mount Rushmore presidents: Dean Malissa, who portrays George Washington at Mount Vernon; Gib Young, who portrays Theodore Roosevelt in Indiana; and Fritz Klein, who portrays Abraham Lincoln in Illinois. We appeared as ghosts of these past residents of the president's house for a daylong Halloween party. Over the years there have been many stories of the White House being haunted by past presidents.

Throughout the day, as the families of Congress and the White House staff went from room to room on the first floor enjoying various vignettes of White House lore, we four impersonators stood by our respective formal state portraits and brought them to life.

Later in the evening, with fewer visitors in the White House, the four of us frequently had the entire first floor to ourselves. It was hauntingly surreal.

Construction of the White House was not completed in time for George Washington to live there. John Adams was its first resident, moving into the drafty new structure in November 1800. He lived there for little more than four months! President Jefferson prevented his predecessor from remaining longer when he won the highly contentious presidential election of 1800.

I sat alone in the Green Room that Halloween knowing that over two hundred years ago it was President Jefferson's formal dining room. I realized too that the state dining room was originally President Jefferson's office. What muses were fluttering about that evening to excite my imagination! Little wonder it is said that President Nixon was seen speaking with portraits of past presidents. So did I that Halloween.

PART III: LEGACIES

To visit the White House, whether in person or persona, substantiates the fact that the president's house truly belongs to the American people. The president is the chief magistrate of our federal government, as Jefferson referred to the office, and always a servant of the people. The people have every right, as they did

▸ THE WHITE HOUSE

even on Halloween, to enjoy the president's house, to be inspired as I was by the relics of American history—the Lansdowne Washington portrait, the John Adams coffeepot, the Monroe medicine chest. All these relics belong to the people as well. Though we have cordoned off much of the surrounding area of the White House and a portion of Pennsylvania Avenue to protect the building and the grounds, let alone the people who live and work there, the fact remains that it belongs to the American people.

PART III: LEGACIES

In the White House's Red Room.

In the Peaks of Otter in the Blue Ridge Mountains, which Jefferson thought were the highest on the east coast.

TRAVELING

Jefferson traveled more extensively throughout Europe than in his own country. He never went south of the Virginia-Carolina line nor west into the Shenandoah Valley. He did travel as far west as Rockfish Gap in the Blue Ridge Mountains and to what is now known as the Jefferson Pools, which are part of the Homestead resort near Covington, Virginia, but he never ventured farther west than that. His farthest northern travels took him to Newport, Rhode Island, and Portsmouth, New Hampshire. He traveled on Long Island when he went on a fishing trip with George Washington and Alexander Hamilton up the east coast, all of

At Versailles, outside of Paris, on a trip with Colonial Williamsburg donors.

them taking time to inspect one of our nation's first lighthouses at Montauk Point.

In May 2012, Colonial Williamsburg's Cultural Expeditions toured "Jefferson's Virginia." Our stops included Tuckahoe, Monticello, Poplar Forest, and the University of Virginia. The Jefferson tour of Virginia provided an opportunity for many people to realize the rural aspect of Jefferson's life. He was born on a farm of yeoman stock, and he considered himself essentially a farmer through his entire life. The trip made clear the conflicts

PART III: LEGACIES

between Jefferson and Alexander Hamilton. In his first inaugural address, Jefferson encouraged the pursuit of agriculture and "commerce as its handmaid." He was skeptical of corporate bodies, accounting houses, and, of course, large private banking institutions, which he considered more dangerous to liberty than standing armies.

Throughout the years portraying Jefferson, I've also had the opportunity to visit places Jefferson never saw but knew about. In particular, I have visited many of the natural marvels recorded by the Lewis and Clark expedition, which was commissioned by President Jefferson in 1803. Jefferson wrote that, were it not for the shackles of administration, he would have been immediately on that expedition. Jefferson excitedly received many items sent back to him by the expedition, such as a buffalo robe and seed and plant specimens. During 2003–2006, I was invited in persona to attend many signature events during the bicentennial of the Lewis and Clark expedition. What would Jefferson have thought had he had the chance to see the many magnificent wonders of nature far to the west beyond the Blue Ridge Mountains?

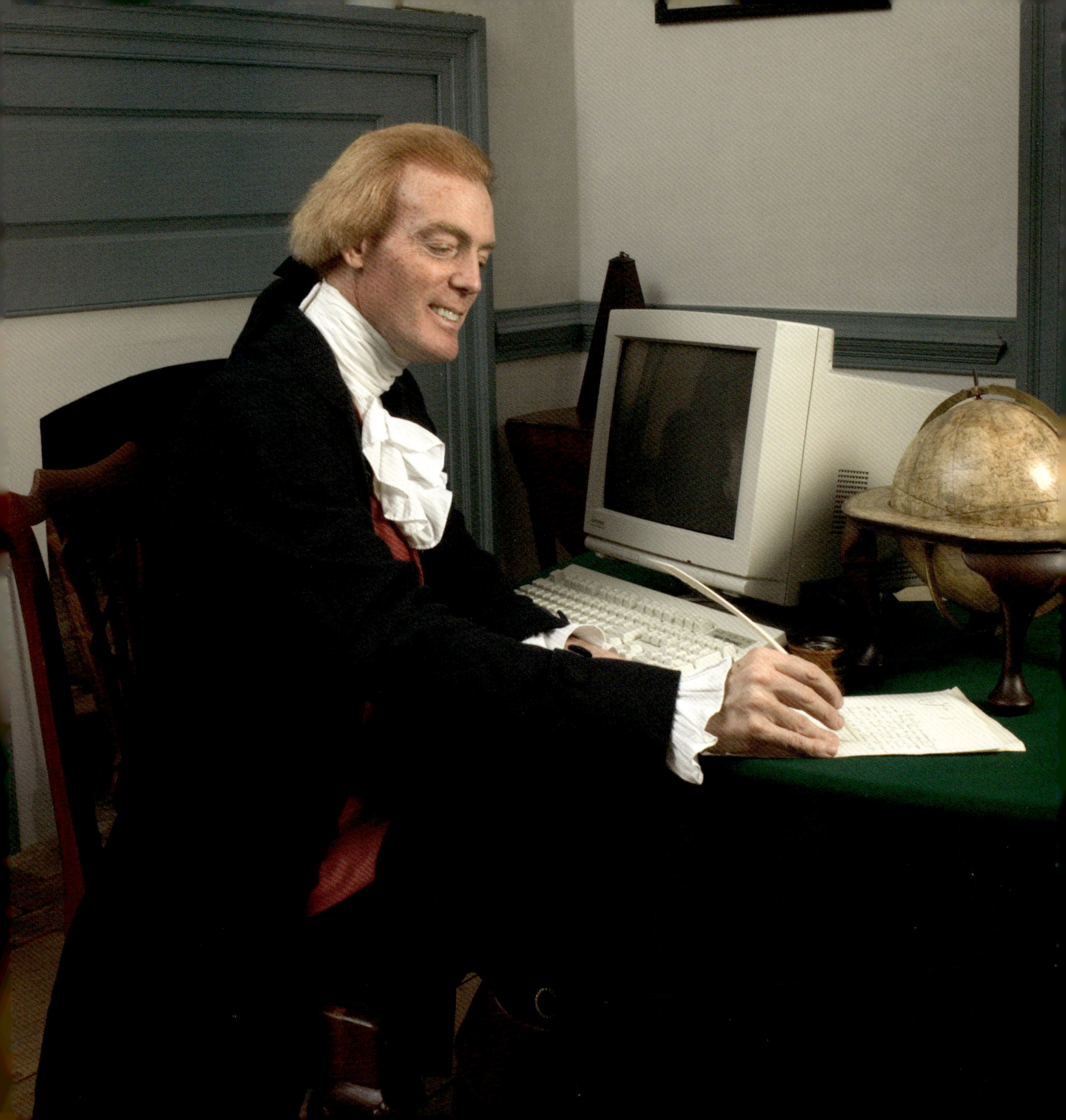

EDUCATION

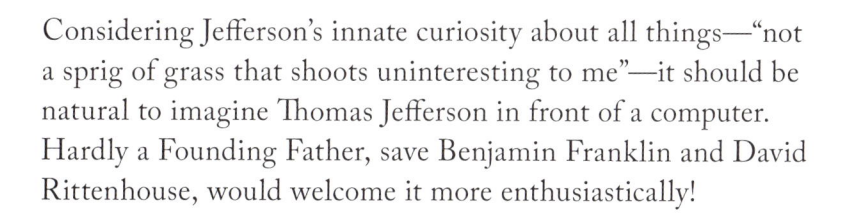

Considering Jefferson's innate curiosity about all things—"not a sprig of grass that shoots uninteresting to me"—it should be natural to imagine Thomas Jefferson in front of a computer. Hardly a Founding Father, save Benjamin Franklin and David Rittenhouse, would welcome it more enthusiastically!

When Jefferson arrived in the urban setting of Williamsburg to attend William and Mary in March 1760, he was very much a product of frontier country life. In Virginia's capital city, truly a college town, Jefferson formally began a more worldly education that continued to benefit him when he later set out on his European travels, as well as throughout his life. The creation of libraries in which to house human knowledge was always one of Jefferson's most fervent interests. Beginning with the inheritance of his father's small library at Shadwell, Jefferson created two extensive storehouses of human knowledge for himself. Had computers existed as a means to further his education, he would surely have embraced them too. He may even have had his own ideas for how we might further improve upon them.

Amongst Jefferson's teachers, the one whom he recognized more than others for opening his mind to greater enlightenment and happiness was Dr. William Small, professor of natural philosophy at William and Mary. When he was in his late seventies and writing his autobiography, Jefferson wrote of Small that he "probably fixed the destinies of my life" and had "a happy talent of communication, correct and gentlemanly manners, and an enlarged and liberal mind." While a student under Small, Jefferson was often invited to attend musicales and dinners at the Governor's Palace during the administration of royal lieutenant governor Francis Fauquier. He did so in the company of Dr. Small and the gentleman with whom he later read law, George Wythe. Jefferson wrote in his autobiography that he found more good common sense in these conversations than in his entire life. Jefferson referred to the happy gathering of Small, Fauquier, Wythe, and himself as a "parti quarré."

PART III: LEGACIES

At Colonial Williamsburg's Bruton Heights School Education Center.

These occasions of elegant enlightened conversation, beginning in his college years in Williamsburg, provided for Jefferson a foundation of history, science, and the arts and also fostered the cultivation of the art of diplomacy through good manners. These experiences carried him in fine form as he later sat thoroughly engaged in conversations with enlightenment thinkers from around the world—in Annapolis, Philadelphia, New York, Boston, Paris, Bordeaux, Beaune, Avignon, Arles, Marseille, Nice, Turin, Milan, Como, Genoa, Strasbourg, Amsterdam,

PART III: LEGACIES

Mannheim, Frankfurt, Heidelberg, London, Blenheim, and Stratford-upon-Avon.

In the autumn of 2006, *The Colbert Report* invited three Jefferson interpreters to appear on the program without the knowledge that the others would be present. I was one of the three. None of us had any idea that Stephen Colbert intended to provoke us to contend with each other. Yet quite the opposite occurred. Our common knowledge and regard for Jefferson's good manners prompted congenial rather than divisive responses. As a result, Mr. Colbert was forced to edit and "twistify"—to use a word Jefferson himself created to describe how news writers twist the truth—the recordings. Ironically, Colbert has a passion for and great knowledge of history.

Reading the law under George Wythe, Jefferson learned not only the foundations of English common law but also the precepts, precedents, and spirit of law throughout the history of Western civilization. He learned the Code of Justinian, the first civil body of law, drawn up in the sixth century, commissioned by Roman emperor Justinian I, declaring that in natural law everyone is born free. Such wisdom of the ancient world had an influence on the drafting of the Declaration of Independence. In addition, Jefferson became familiar with the writings of the seventeenth-century English philosopher John Locke, whose thinking also found its way into our Declaration.

▸ EDUCATION

In the spring of 1766, at the age of twenty-three, Jefferson first traveled to Philadelphia, the financial and cultural center of colonial America. At the time, it was the largest city in North America. He went there to be inoculated against smallpox. As was customary with the eighteenth-century process of inoculation, Jefferson fell ill, and during the course of his recovery he initiated several lifelong friendships, one of whom was with Charles Thomson, who at the time was a Latin teacher at the Public Grammar School in Philadelphia and later its headmaster. The Public Grammar School later became the William Penn Charter School, which I attended and from which I graduated in 1971.

Charles Thomson later became the secretary of the Continental Congress from its very first session in September 1774 through the declaration of our independence in 1776 and on through the Confederation Congress under the Articles of Confederation to the first Congress under our Constitution in 1789. Mr. Thomson's name is the only other name to appear with John Hancock in the first printings of our Declaration of Independence. In becoming acquainted with Thomson and other gentlemen in Philadelphia, Jefferson was introduced to urban public schools, albeit for families who had the means, as well as a city in which religion was practiced freely. Most profoundly, in Philadelphia Jefferson was introduced to the first slave emancipation society in the Western world.

PART III: LEGACIES

After recovering from the smallpox inoculation and returning to Virginia, Jefferson was like a bee charged with honey: Why not pursue change for a more enlightened society in Virginia by helping create laws that would establish a system of schools and freedom for religion and especially new laws to end slavery? Why not put the law to good use for improving mankind?

Later, after the colonies had declared independence, Jefferson would work with George Wythe, Thomas Ludwell Lee, George Mason, and Edmund Pendleton to create 126 revisions of the British laws of Virginia. Amongst these were bill no. 79 for a "Diffusion of Knowledge," no. 82 for "Establishing Religious Freedom," and no. 51 to end the importation of slaves to Virginia and allow a master to free his slaves. Gone were references to the monarchy. All of these extraordinary innovations by Jefferson in the legal history of Virginia, let alone in the first years of our young nation, have been incorporated during the last twenty-five years into a range of programming at Colonial Williamsburg, as well as into outreach programs and donor trips.

SLAVERY

There has never been a question in my mind that Jefferson was deeply devoted to, and at the same time conflicted over, ending slavery.

Through nearly four decades of interpreting Thomas Jefferson, the two foremost subjects brought before me in persona are slavery and religion. Naturally, many want to understand how the author of the Declaration of Independence could write what he did and yet own slaves. Others are more interested in proving Jefferson a hypocrite and a liar.

With Lydia Broadnax (portrayed by Katrinah Lewis), who was owned and then freed by George Wythe.

My response has always been to provide context by explaining how many Americans in Jefferson's day, especially Jefferson, were caught up in this conflict. Our nation began as a slave-owning nation and continued so through Jefferson's life and for thirty-four years afterward.

After a lifetime of study on Jefferson and his times, I sincerely believe he meant what he wrote in the Declaration—that all men, meaning the family of man, including women, are created equal. Not that man is created equal in face or form. Nor are we all created equal in ability. But we are all born free in nature.

Jefferson was passionate in his beliefs. He abhorred the institution of slavery. He understood well that the acts of hostility and aggression against enslaved people for so long could not be forgotten, and he acknowledged the corrupting effects of slavery upon slave and master alike. Jefferson's servants and slaves must have questioned his Declaration of Independence, and I believe Jefferson talked with them about it—describing it as a declaration of hope for the future that could not be achieved overnight.

Even before the Declaration, in March 1770 Jefferson made his first statement that "under the law of nature, all men are born free" during his defense of Samuel Howell, who was being held in indentured servitude because his grandmother was white and his grandfather was black. Virginia law required the children of a white woman and a black man to serve a term of indentured servitude but did not mention the grandchildren of such unions. In *Samuel Howell v. Wade Netherland*, George Wythe was the prosecuting attorney, and Jefferson lost the case. This was the subject of a program reenacted in the Capitol titled "Under the Laws of Nature," which we presented in the mid to late 1990s.

As Annette Gordon-Reed and Peter S. Onuf have expressed in their book, *"Most Blessed of the Patriarchs,"* Jefferson saw himself and his efforts to abolish slavery with respect to that biblical reference—the obligation of every generation to make a better world for the next generation. Jefferson at twenty-six, when elected to his first public office as a burgess, took the initiative to begin a debate to end the importation of slaves. At thirty-one, he condemned slavery in his *Summary View of the Rights of British America* printed in Williamsburg. He stated therein: "The abolition of domestic slavery is the great object of desire in those colonies, where it was unhappily introduced in their infant state. But previous to the enfranchisement of the slaves we have, it is necessary to exclude all further importations from Africa."

At thirty-six, he introduced bill no. 51 amongst his 126 revisals to end the importation of slaves to Virginia and to allow masters to free all their slaves. Jefferson himself could not afford to free his slaves. By the time he returned from the years in France and began nearly two more decades in public office, Jefferson's debt

Reading the Declaration of Independence.

accumulated rapidly, and his slaves became the collateral to his many creditors.

Jefferson continued to pursue this dramatic effort to bring about the end of slavery when in the spring of 1784 he was invited by Congress to chair a committee to draft a bill for establishing new states out of the Northwest Territory. Jefferson included in the Land Ordinance of 1784 a provision to prohibit slavery in the new states, but that clause was defeated by one vote. The later Northwest Ordinance of 1787, however, did ban slavery north of the Ohio River.

As he grew older and into his retirement years, Jefferson tried to encourage his "people" (he rarely referred to them as slaves) to cultivate their own gardens and sell the produce for their own profit. He helped by selling some of their products for them. Difficult as it is for our modern sensitivities to comprehend, Jefferson accepted that, under the law of his times, enslaved people were his property. Though this too is difficult for us to comprehend, he also referred to them as his family.

It remains very difficult for us, and for me as an interpreter, to grasp fully the inhumanity of slavery. Today as Americans, we are no longer living in a time and culture that sanctions slavery. However, we still have a long way to go towards providing more equal opportunity and eradicating racial bias.

Jefferson's first trip to Philadelphia opened his mind to Quaker humanitarian principles that were actively manifest in the City of Brotherly Love. The Quaker view of the divine in all creatures must have provided an imaginative vision for a world very different from the preachings from the pulpits of the Church of England.

In October 2012 I was invited by my alma mater, the William Penn Charter School, to appear in persona for the school's 325th anniversary and to comment upon Jefferson's statement that William Penn was perhaps the greatest lawgiver the world ever produced.

Jefferson wrote this comment in September 1825 in response to a letter he received from Peter Stephen Du Ponceau, a successful attorney and French immigrant living in Philadelphia. Du Ponceau wrote to Jefferson to invite him to a celebration in Philadelphia commemorating William Penn's first step on American soil. Jefferson wrote that old age and ill health would prevent him from traveling so far again but that it may be said in his absence that he considered William Penn "the greatest lawgiver the world has produced" because he more than anyone first established in this new world freedom for religion, public schools, and the first slave emancipation society in the Western world.

William Penn, like Jefferson, was a slave owner. Penn, like Jefferson, took steps early on toward ending slavery. Efforts for a better world in the midst of inhumanity and injustice must begin at a starting point.

The American Revolution, Jefferson believed, would prompt all eyes to begin to see the inherent rights of man. He believed "knowledge is power…knowledge is happiness." Jefferson's bill no. 79, for universal education, never passed in its entirety in his lifetime. Imagine what a difference its passage may have had, especially to enlighten many to the ills of slavery—morally, politically, and economically.

Nevertheless, we still find it difficult to reconcile the enlightened Jefferson with his *Notes on the State of Virginia*. Our concerns remain over Jefferson's descriptions of the racial diversity in the Virginia of his day. In particular, his descriptions of the physical traits, general personality, and intellect of Africans are overtly racist and deplorable. As an interpreter, however, I strive to portray Jefferson in the manner in which he portrayed himself. So as Jefferson, I will often emphasize how he warned that these observations were suspicions rather than definitive fact and required further scrutiny. Jefferson intended Notes for private printing and circulation and admonished anyone who suggested that it be used as educational curriculum against doing so.

Growing up, I often felt the confines of another era within my own family. My father was born in 1894. He knew both his grandfathers, who were Confederate veterans. I grew up knowing that my great-grandfathers had been slave owners. Though I was born and reared in Philadelphia, I witnessed the Jim Crow laws of the later nineteenth century still in effect when we visited our southern relations during the 1950s and 1960s. I am thankful today that we are emerging from our shells of silence over our nation's past. We are having more discussions about what it means to be an American no matter where one's family is from and what their lineage is. Education and the pursuit of science help immensely in this effort. DNA revelations are bringing the family of man closer together. My own DNA testing has revealed extended cousins with both white and black blood. But, then, isn't it all simply the collective blood of the human race? Jefferson pondered these same questions in his own times.

With manservant Jupiter (portrayed by Richard Josey).

THE BIBLE

My lifetime of Jefferson studies and interpretation has convinced me that Jefferson was an ardent follower of scientific investigation and discovery who remained a very spiritual man as well throughout his life. Unfortunately, for generations his writings on the separation between church and state have too often been misconstrued to imply that he was impious, heretical, and possibly an atheist. Nothing could be further from the truth with respect to Jefferson's communion with his maker. His statement "We are not afraid to follow truth wherever it may lead" is not a contradiction to his comment "Question with boldness even the existence of a god because, if there be one, he must more approve the homage of reason than that of blindfolded fear."

In reply to a letter that President Jefferson received in late 1801 from a group of Baptist preachers in Danbury, Connecticut, who cared not to pay a church tax or levy to the established Congregational Church, he wrote to the Danbury Baptist Association, "Believing…that religion is a matter which lies solely between man and his God…I contemplate with sovereign reverence that act of the whole American people which declared that *their* legislature should 'make no law respecting an establishment of religion, or prohibiting the free exercise thereof,' thus building a wall of separation between church and state."

The connector "between" rather than the phrase "separation of" is crucial for understanding Jefferson's principle of freedom for religion—not freedom from religion. He never even implied that religion ought to be separated from our lives or from the lives of those we elect or appoint to public office. However, Patrick Henry disagreed with Jefferson's approach to the subject, particularly Jefferson's Bill for Establishing Religious Freedom.

Jefferson believed that separating civil and ecclesiastical authorities provided more freedom for both. He believed in freedom *for* religion, not freedom *from* religion. The title of the bill Jefferson introduced in Virginia was the Bill *for* Establishing Religious

Freedom. After seven years of contentious debate in the Virginia House of Delegates, it was passed in 1786 as the Virginia Statute *for* Religious Freedom.

Jefferson, early in life, had inscribed on his watch fob seal "Rebellion to tyrants is obedience to God." Cut on the inside of the Jefferson Memorial in Washington, dedicated in 1943 on the two-hundredth anniversary of Jefferson's birth, are the resounding words that he wrote to Benjamin Rush in 1800: "I have sworn upon the altar of God eternal hostility against every form of tyranny over the mind of man."

Jefferson was a man of science but also of faith. He had faith in the power of mankind to improve the world.

In his autobiography, he wrote that the argument over religion remains one of "the severest contests in which I have ever been engaged." In his correspondence, Jefferson wrote, "I never go to bed without an hour or half hour's previous reading of something moral, whereon to ruminate in the intervals of sleep."

Throughout his adult life, Jefferson remained on the vestry at St. Anne's Parish in Albemarle County, where he was baptized into the Church of England as an infant. He supported the Bible Society of Virginia, which distributed Bibles free of charge. He donated funds to support the building of the first church in

PART III: LEGACIES

Charlottesville. This was someone who made an effort to attend services every Sunday, and if he wasn't near an Episcopal church, he would go to a Methodist camp or a Presbyterian or Quaker meeting or even a Catholic chapel. He went to a Jewish temple in Philadelphia and later in Newport, Rhode Island. He also attended services regularly in Washington, D.C., during his presidency.

Another victim of "twistifications" (a word coined by Jefferson) of historical fact is what has become known as the "Jefferson Bible." Mr. Jefferson did not write his own version of the Bible. What has come to be known as the Jefferson Bible is the title Congress affixed to his personal scholarship when they published it in 1905. The project is the result of Jefferson's study of translations of the four Gospels in Greek, Latin, French, and English to compile the life and words of Jesus by way of the eyewitness accounts in the Gospels. Jefferson began his study during the first years of his presidency and later titled it "The Life and Morals of Jesus of Nazareth." Jefferson's purpose was for his better understanding of the teachings of Jesus. The Jefferson Bible was not, as his critics have said, blasphemy. It did not denigrate the moral lessons taught by Jesus. Rather, it was an effort to get at what Jesus actually said.

When I am interpreting Jefferson and someone asks, "Tell me about your Bible," I answer, "I beg your pardon. I trust I am not considered so presumptuous as to write a Bible. What you are perhaps referring to is my scholarly investigation of what Jesus was known to have said."

Many people will say, "What do you mean by 'what he was known to have said'? It's all in the Bible."

To which I then answer, "Which one? The Catholic Bible or the Protestant Bible? The teachings of Jesus have been published in many different versions, translations, and languages. And Jesus himself did not write down his own words."

Jefferson remarked in his correspondence, "To the corruptions of Christianity, I am indeed opposed, but not to the genuine precepts of Jesus himself. I am a Christian in the only sense in which he [Jesus] wished anyone to be, sincerely attached to his doctrines, in preference to all others, ascribing to himself every human excellence, and believing he never claimed any other."

We learn from Jefferson little more about his actual religious opinions. He decidedly wants it that way. He wrote to Richard Rush in May 1813, "The subject of religion, a subject on which I have ever been most scrupulously reserved. I have considered it as a matter between every man and his maker, in which no other, and far less the public, had a right to intermeddle."

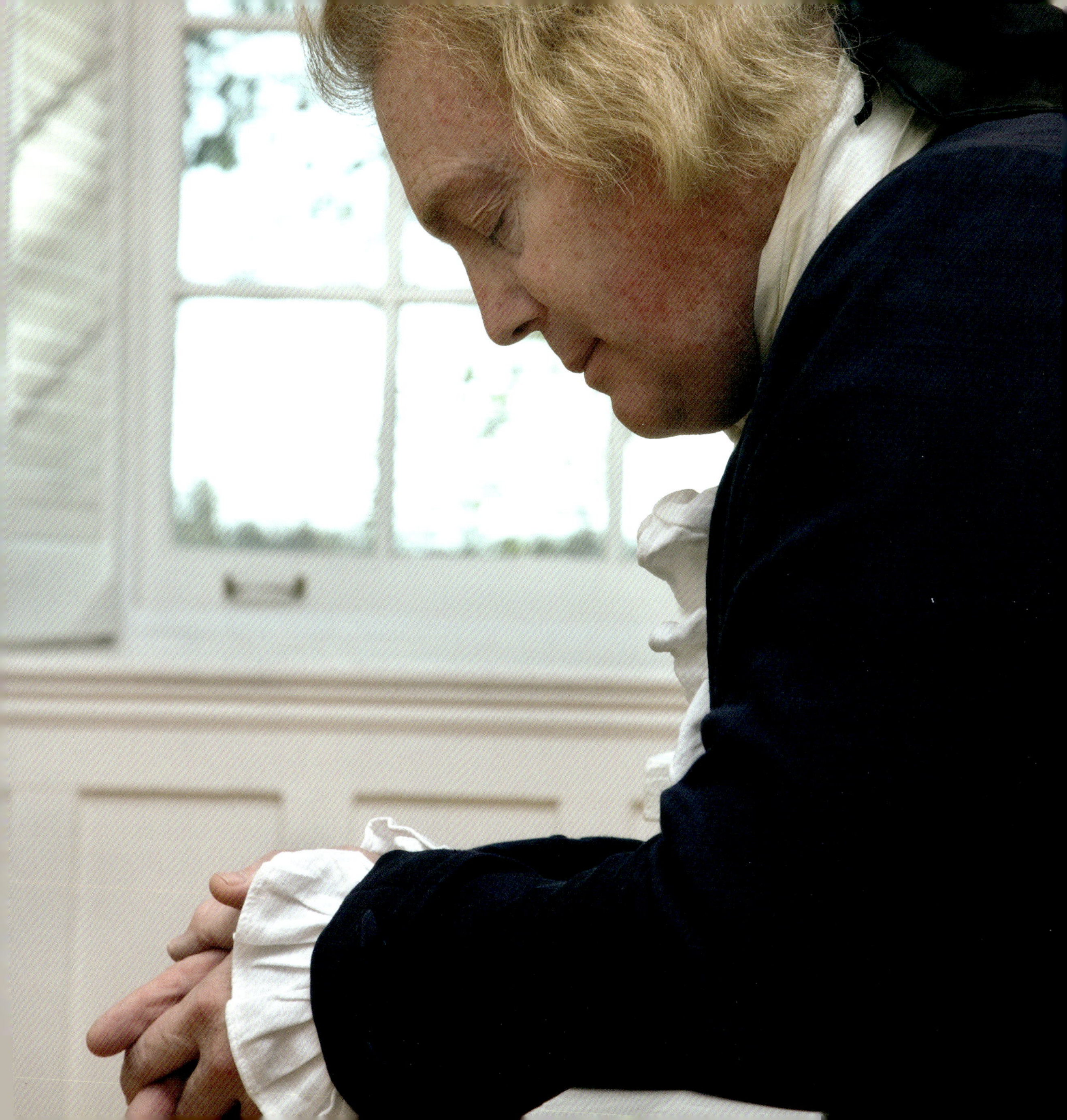

SOME FINAL THOUGHTS

Over two hundred and fifty years ago, many in the college town of Williamsburg, the colonial capital of Virginia, were curious to know more about this eldest son of the late renowned surveyor Col. Peter Jefferson of Shadwell, from what was then the Virginia wilderness of Albemarle County. As a young student at the College of William and Mary and through the following twenty years as a young man reading law, practicing law, elected to his first public office, and finally elected as the second governor of the new Commonwealth of Virginia, Jefferson remained an object of interest. Indeed, every day since he shed his mortal coil in 1826, the questions about him have multiplied.

These questions have provoked many interpretations of his life. These have taken the forms of the reclaiming of his homes at

Monticello and Poplar Forest, numerous biographies (the first in 1829), collections of his papers (the first in 1827), novels, theses, and commentaries in pamphlets, magazines, and newspapers and on radio, television, and the internet. Oddly, Jefferson has been represented but a few times in stage plays, film, and television.

Have we really come to know him? His biographer Dumas Malone said, in a private interview shortly after the sixth and last volume of his work was published in 1979, that even he had not come to know Jefferson entirely. This was the case even after fifty years of studying him.

In or about 1800, during what were several years of acute political divisiveness in our nation, and at a time when Jefferson was contending for the office of the presidency, he wrote, "I have sometimes asked myself whether my country is the better for my having lived at all?" He follows with a list of accomplishments, beginning with his successful efforts to dredge the Rivanna River near his home in his youth, but he says these would have been done anyway. After emerging as the victor in the bitter election of 1800, Jefferson declared in his inaugural address "a sincere consciousness that the task is above my talents."

Jefferson's self-doubts, despite his remarkable talents and undeniable legacy, ought perhaps to prompt us to look in the mirror at our own foibles and failures. They are just one of many daunting challenges facing the Jefferson interpreter, who can sometimes feel overwhelmed by conflicting images and information.

Despite Jefferson's many contradictions, historical interpreters are fortunate that Jefferson's friends and enemies and Jefferson himself have left us much about his life and times.

Contrary to the image of him as a reticent, restrained, retiring, cerebral, and distant "American Sphinx," eyewitness accounts do not generally present him as a shy and inept public speaker. While he may have been uncomfortable before large audiences and preferred to read his speeches before handing them over to the press for public scrutiny, he was quite comfortable in the company of his family and friends. In more intimate scenarios, he was known to be loquacious, inviting, questioning. As Senator William Maclay of Pennsylvania remarked, "He spoke almost without ceasing. But even his discourse partook of his personal demeanor. It was loose and rambling, and yet he scattered information wherever he went, and some even brilliant sentiments sparkled from him."

Benjamin Franklin recalled later in life that, during the sessions of the Continental Congress when he sat next to Mr. Jefferson, he knew him only to utter but a few words. Perhaps this was an indication that Jefferson was deep in thought and hard at work. Our very first eyewitness account of a young Thomas Jefferson is quite different. In the early spring of 1782, the French nobleman

François Jean de Beauvoir, Marquis de Chastellux, having been present at the Battle of Yorktown the previous fall and having then spent the winter in Williamsburg, set out on a journey through western Virginia. He visited Jefferson at Monticello. Though he initially found the thirty-nine-year-old Jefferson "grave and even cold; but I had no sooner spent two hours with him than I felt as if we had spent our whole lives together. Walking, the library—and above all, conversation which was always varied, always interesting…all these made my four days spent at Monticello seem like four minutes." Chastellux also wrote, "I perceive that my journal is something like the conversation I had with Mr. Jefferson. I pass from one object to another, and forget myself as I write, as it happened not unfrequently in his society." Surely, it is the image of the inquisitive, energetic, engaging, respectful, and well-mannered individual that best serves in presenting Mr. Jefferson to the public, especially with a recognition of his droll and subdued sense of humor.

Many recorded how, when they visited Monticello, Jefferson would receive them with gentlemanly manners and good humor. Jefferson learned manners in his youth and passed them on to his sixteen-year-old grandson, Thomas Jefferson Randolph, and I think it appropriate to close with Jefferson's own words of advice:

> A determination never to do what is wrong, prudence, and good humor will go far towards securing to you the

estimation of the world.... I have mentioned good humor as one of the preservatives of our peace and tranquility. It is among the most effectual, and its effect is so well-imitated and aided artificially by politeness that this also becomes an acquisition of first-rate value. In truth, politeness is artificial good humor; it covers the natural want of it and ends by rendering habitual a substitute nearly equivalent to the real virtue. It is the practice of sacrificing to those whom we meet in society all the little conveniences and preferences which will gratify them and deprive us of nothing worth a moment's consideration; it is the giving a pleasing and flattering turn to our expressions which will conciliate others and make them pleased with us as well as themselves. How cheap a price for the good will of another!

ACKNOWLEDGMENTS

With many thanks to my loving parents, the late William David Barker and Anabel Gault Manderson Barker, who introduced me to the wonders of history and will always remain my first loves and models of good manners; Scott and Debra Duncan, who supported this book; Bob and Marion Wilson, who believed in me during my first year at Colonial Williamsburg; Roy Underwood and Bob Wilburn, who helped bring me into the fold of the Colonial Williamsburg family; Colin and Nancy Campbell, whose example of enlightened leadership will remain for me a beacon of John D. Rockefeller Jr.'s vision; the late Abby O'Neill, whose wisdom and charm helped keep her grandfather's dream alive and relevant for me; Don and Elaine Bogus, ever bringing people together in true Jeffersonian manner; Forrest Williamson; Mitchell and Elisabeth Reiss, for welcoming me to remain in persona as "vintage Jefferson" well after passing the age, thirty-seven years old, when Mr. Jefferson left Williamsburg; Cary Carson and Jim Horn, whose happy guidance and support keeps history alive and engaged; Dr. Barbara B. Oberg, former editor of *The Papers of Thomas Jefferson,* whose sensitivity to the context of Jefferson's words helps them to breathe ever renewed and relevant; the late historian, author, and teacher Alf Mapp, whose encouragement provided me with comfort and purpose; Susan R. Stein and Lucia C. Stanton of Monticello, whose works remain bibles of Jefferson's world for me; Dr. Larry J. Sabato, University of Virginia professor, who exemplifies the integrity and open mind of the "father of the University of Virginia"; Chip Stokes and the Jefferson Legacy Foundation for their gift of the perennial production of Howard Ginsberg's wonderful play *Jefferson & Adams*; Abigail Schumann, Emily James, Richard Schumann, and Mark Schneider, my trusted coworkers at Colonial Williamsburg for over twenty years; Bill Weldon; former teachers Joan Reardon, Carol DiJoseph, Russell Faber, Effie Coganower, Margaret Worrall, and Mary Ellen Rockefeller, whose teaching of history was always factual and inspiring; Kurt Smith, delightful friend and compatriot; and, not least in recognition, the late Bill Sommerfield, Ralph Archbold, and Carl Gatter, inspirations and exceptional examples of the art of first-person historical interpretation; Linda Rowe, Colonial Williamsburg's historian emeritus; and my lifelong friends David Kennedy and Bart Schenkel, who have known from our childhood that I am a storyteller.